MURLE JONES

The BEAttitudes

The Be Attitudes
Trilogy Christian Publishers A Wholly Owned Subsidiary of Trinity Broadcasting Network
2442 Michelle Drive Tustin, CA 92780
Copyright © 2024 by Murle Jones

Unless otherwise indicated, all Scripture quotations are taken from the King James Version of the Bible. Public domain. Scripture quotations marked AMP are taken from the Amplified® Bible (AMP), Copyright © 2015 by The Lockman Foundation. Used by permission. www.lockman.org. Scripture quotations marked ESV are taken from the ESV® Bible (The Holy Bible, English Standard Version®), copyright © 2001 by Crossway Bibles, a publishing ministry of Good News Publishers. ©All rights reserved. Scripture quotations marked NIV are taken from the Holy Bible, New International Version®, NIV®. Copyright © 1973, 1978, 1984, 2011 by Biblica, Inc.™ Used by permission of Zondervan. All rights reserved worldwide. www.zondervan.com. The "NIV" and "New International Version" are trademarks registered in the United States Patent and Trademark Office by Biblica, Inc.™ Scripture quotations marked NKJV are taken from the New King James Version®. Copyright © 1982 by Thomas Nelson. Used by permission. All rights reserved. Scripture quotations marked NLT are taken from the Holy Bible, New Living Translation, copyright © 1996, 2004, 2015 by Tyndale House Foundation. Used by permission of Tyndale House Publishers, Inc., Carol Stream, Illinois 60188. All rights reserved.

No part of this book may be reproduced, stored in a retrieval system, or transmitted by any means without written permission from the author. All rights reserved. Printed in the USA.

Rights Department, 2442 Michelle Drive, Tustin, CA 92780.

Trilogy Christian Publishing/TBN and colophon are trademarks of Trinity Broadcasting Network.

For information about special discounts for bulk purchases, please contact Trilogy Christian Publishing.

Trilogy Disclaimer: The views and content expressed in this book are those of the author and may not necessarily reflect the views and doctrine of Trilogy Christian Publishing or the Trinity Broadcasting Network.

10 9 8 7 6 5 4 3 2 1

Library of Congress Cataloging-in-Publication Data is available.
ISBN: 979-8-89041-714-5
E-ISBN: 979-8-89041-715-2

Dedication

This book is dedicated to my Father in heaven, who never gave up on me. Despite my fears and propensity to second-guess myself, He has always encouraged me and confirmed to me how much He loves and adores me. His steadfast love through the Holy Spirit has guided me throughout the years and brought me to this point in my life, when my total trust lies with Him. Wherever He leads, I will follow. My life is in His hands. The apostle Paul referred to it like this: "I am crucified with Christ: nevertheless I live; yet not I, but Christ liveth in me: and the life which I now live in the flesh I live by the faith of the Son of God, who loved me, and gave himself for me" (Galatians 2:20). Thank You, Lord, and I still say "yes."

Table of Contents

Foreword by Timothy Jones 9

Acknowledgments. 11

Prologue 13

1   Blessings of the Kingdom of Heaven 19

2   Comforting Thoughts 45

3   The Inheritance of the Meek 53

4   Filled to the Brim. 61

5   Unlimited Mercy 71

6   Pure Eyesight. 81

7   Blessings of Peace 93

8   Righteous Blessings, Destiny Helpers. 127

9   Savory Seasonings. 139

10   Beam Me Up 149

11   The Light of His Glory 159

Comprehension Review 177

Epilogue 185

About the Author. 189

Notes. 198

Ministry Information. 201

Foreword

I was going through the toughest time of my life. I wanted to give up on my marriage and myself, and I even was ready to give up on God. When Murle Jones asked me to write the foreword to her book, I did not realize God was going to give me the answers to my agony of heart. This book, *The Be Attitudes*, showed me that the attitude I had about my situation was all wrong. As I read this book, tears flowed, my eyes opened, and my heart was enlightened. To my surprise, God in His essence was bringing healing to me through this book. *The Be Attitudes* was written under His anointing power, through this woman of God, Murle Jones. I thank God for urging her to write this book, as it changed my outlook, my focus, and I guess you can say, even my life. It placed me back on track with God and with his Son, Jesus, and it reunited me with the Holy Spirit. I urge you to read this book carefully alongside God's Word. *The Be Attitudes* is life-changing and inspired from the very heart of God. You will be glad you have read it and incorporated its principles into your life.

Timothy Jones
Minister, Church of God in Christ
Memphis, Tennessee

Acknowledgments

I would like to acknowledge my son, Timothy, and my daughter Taketha for always sowing into the ministry, as well as my daughter Mesha', for sowing into my personal life. Their support kept me encouraged to press on until the victory was won. I thank my family for loving me and believing in the God I serve. They have believed in the call on my life, trusting my prayers, and as a result, we have experienced divine encounters, interventions, and miracles in our lives.

Thank you, as well, to Donnie McClurkin and all the prophets who spoke of the books that would come out of my life. Thank you to my sister, Catherine, for introducing me to my Lord and Savior, Jesus Christ. Thank you to my spiritual father and mother, the late Bishop G.E. Patterson and Louise Patterson, who taught me "Jesus Christ crucified and never, ever compromised."

Thank You, Lord, for the call upon my life, for Your choice of me, and for refining me for Your purpose. Thank You for Your steadfast love, forgiveness, mercy, and grace, and for being a trusted Father who knows what is best for my life. The many trials and tribulations You allowed in my life taught me how to trust in You. I learned the *How to BE Attitudes* through every situation You brought into my life.

Prologue

During a battle with COVID, my life was drastically changed. For about a six- to eight-week time frame, I found myself barely able to get around, and I had breathing issues off and on until the Lord touched my body and healed me. What should have been the worst time in my life turned out to be the most glorious time ever. Around the beginning of my second week of COVID, I knew I was in trouble. I began to pray a prayer of repentance for every sin—both of commission and of omission—just to make sure I was right before God.

The strangest thing is, while I was contemplating whether I should go to the hospital or stay home, whether I was going to make it or not—because my mind was all over the place—I fell into a trance. It seemed like I was lifted up above my body. I could see myself lying in bed, but I was also looking around, and I could see every room in my house at the same time. I was wondering how my children would divide up my belongings, and how they would cope if I did not make it. They had tried to persuade me to go to the hospital, but I felt the urging of the Holy Spirit to stay home.

Because I didn't want them to become ill, too, I locked my door and would not allow them to come in. I only talked to them by phone and via Facetime. During the time I was in the "trance," I heard the Lord say, *You will not die, but live, and declare the works of the Lord.* (See Psalm 118:17.) I had so many divine encounters over the next few days, I will have to tell you about them in my next book. As a preview, just before the encounters ended, an angel of the Lord told me that my course had changed, that the things I used to do were taking up too much of my time, and the Lord needed me to write down all the things He had placed inside of me so this generation could read and believe. It was strange to me because I had been doing nothing but church work, what I called "ministry." But I learned that too much ministry work could eat up all my time, and the question in my mind immediately was, *Did I leave God out?* I had overextended myself to the point of exhaustion, depletion, and dehydration, which led to a low immune system—and then pneumonia.

I learned these next Scriptures in a tangible way during this time of illness:

> *For he shall give his angels charge over thee, to keep thee in all thy ways. They shall bear thee up in their hands, lest thou dash thy foot against a stone.*
> **—Psalm 91:11–12**

> *Because he hath set his love upon me, therefore will I deliver him: I will set him on high, because he hath known my name.*
> **—Psalm 91:14**

The angels of the Lord do, indeed, encamp around

PROLOGUE

those who love God (Psalm 34:7). Although I believed these Scriptures, they are now etched in my heart and mind because of my divine encounters. The Lord's instruction was to let the light of God shine through my life in this season through my writing. I thought my first book would be concerning my bout with COVID and the angelic visits I experienced, but as I was reading the gospel of Matthew, the Lord told me this would be the first book of divine revelations that I am to write. My eyes began to open into another lens, and what you are about to read is the revelation the Holy Spirit shared with me on this journey of authorship.

As my eyes were opened into the realm of the Spirit and the revelation He was sharing, I could see Jesus on the mountain, teaching the Beatitudes to His disciples and all who had followed Him. I have read these Scriptures many times and have heard messages preached many more times about the Beatitudes, but never had I seen this light of the Word before. Neither had I realized the depth of the teaching Jesus was sharing. My heart began to fill with the love He had while sharing these truths and His concern for their lives. Those who were listening were about to experience a whole new life as they journeyed with Him. Our lives, too, will change as we begin our own personal journeys walking with Him and allowing God to use our lives as He did.

THE BE ATTITUDES

The blessing of the L<small>ORD</small>, it maketh rich, and he addeth no sorrow with it.

—Proverbs 10:22

Yielding ourselves to the call of God brings blessings upon our lives. Submitting ourselves to His Word and living a godly life as we obey Him renders an opened heaven of blessings:

Blessings of the Kingdom

Blessings of love and comfort

Blessings of an eternal inheritance while still on earth (financial provision)

Blessings of divine encounters with God

Blessings of reward

This book will prove to be a great read, helping you to experience God's glory and power. Be prepared to release this glory to others as they ask about the light they see in you. Stay posted for my next book, as well. It is an exciting time in the Kingdom of God! The world is about to see and hear what has not been seen before in this last outpouring of His glory before His return.

Eye hath not seen, nor ear heard, neither have entered into the heart of man, the things which God hath prepared for them that love him.

—1 Corinthians 2:9

PROLOGUE

God bless!

***

Father, I pray that while reading this book, all who receive this word will be touched by the glory of the Lord. And as they share it with others, I pray that the light of God will shine to its full capacity and the anointing of the Holy Spirit will fall with signs and wonders, healing, and deliverance—that You might be glorified. I pray that these words will be shared with others through Bible studies to teach these truths that You have revealed. I thank You now for these things, in Jesus' name, amen.

1

Blessings of the Kingdom of Heaven

Let There Be

*And God said, Let there be light:
and there was light.*

—Genesis 1:3

This verse demonstrates the first mention of the word *be* in the Bible. When I read this verse of Scripture, the word *be* stuck out in my mind. Usually when this happens, the Holy Spirit takes me on a journey of revelation knowledge concerning either the mind of God or His Kingdom. In this case, He was revealing God's heart and mind toward His plan of creation and His purpose for those He has created. Let us go on this journey of discovery and revelation of this word, *be*.

THE BE ATTITUDES

One of the present tenses of the word *be* is "(I) am." Reading this definition immediately placed me into the story of Moses in Exodus 3, starting with verses 13 and 14:

And Moses said unto God, Behold, when I come unto the children of Israel, and shall say unto them, The God of your fathers hath sent me unto you; and they shall say to me, What is his name? What shall I say unto them? And God said unto Moses, I AM THAT I AM: and he said, Thus shalt thou say unto the children of Israel, I AM hath sent me unto you.

Some other meanings of the word *be* are "to exist or live," "to take place," "to happen," and "to occur." In the *Encyclopedia Britannica*, the word *be* is used to show the identity of a person or thing, to describe the qualities of a person or thing, to show the condition of a person or thing, or finally, to show the group, class, category, place, situation, or position of a person or thing.

It is these definitions that distinctly line up with the Beatitudes that Jesus spoke of in Matthew 5. We will look deeper into this later.

BLESSINGS OF THE KINGDOM OF HEAVEN

The online *Etymology Dictionary* is one of the most interesting to me because it places the word *be* in a position of being God Himself. It says that the meaning of the word *be* is "I am; I will be, grow, and become." It also includes the words *am*, *are*, *is*, *was*, *were*, *being*, and *been*. Reading those meanings placed me right back again to the time when God told Moses to tell the children of Israel who He was: "I AM THAT I AM." It also reminded me of the attributes of our God; He is the "Alpha and Omega, the beginning and the ending" (Revelation 1:8), and everything in between. I can hear Him saying, "I AM the beginning of all things. I AM a very present help in time of need. I AM at the end of your journey here on earth. I AM life forevermore!"

When I began to look at the steps God took in creation in the book of Genesis, I saw the word *be* all over the place— just by acknowledging what came out of the words, "let there *be*." It was like God was spreading Himself all over the universe! The first "be" concerned light, or illumination. "God is light, and there is no darkness in him at all" (1 John 1:5). So, the first thing God did was to rid the situation of evil and darkness. During the pre-Adamic time, at some point between Genesis 1 and 2, a rebellion took place in heaven, led by Lucifer, one of the archangels whom God had created. Because of the evil and darkness that covered the earth after Satan and the angels that followed Him fell into rebellion, according to Genesis 1, the earth was "without form and void; and darkness was upon the face of the deep. And the Spirit of God moved upon the face of the waters" (verse 2). As I looked a little deeper into the Scriptures, the Holy Spirit revealed to me that the plan of God to renew the earth and bring forth salvation was made in the Spirit realm—in heaven—long before it was ever manifested on the earth.

> *Thy kingdom come, thy will be done in earth, as it is in heaven.*

—Matthew 6:10

In Revelation 12, the apostle John gave a description of the war in heaven that took place between Lucifer and his fallen angels, and the archangel Michael and the hosts of the Lord. Revelation 12:7–11 describes this awesome defeat of Satan and his followers and tells about the coming of salvation through Christ. What really interested me in this passage were verses 1 through 6, as it described the symbolic "woman," who could have represented Eve, Mary, or both; the birth of Christ, the Seed who would bruise Satan's head, as promised in Genesis 3:15; as well as the Church, or Bride, of our Lord. When Satan perceived his demise was near—which included God's plan of salvation and the coming Church—he did everything in his power to stop it. Verse 4 says that with his tail he drew one-third of the stars of heaven and cast them down to the earth; then he stood before the woman who was ready to give birth, to devour the child who was to be born. In verses 13 through 17, Satan cast out of his mouth water, as of a

BLESSINGS OF THE KINGDOM OF HEAVEN

flood, to destroy the woman and her child, but verse 16 says, "The earth helped the woman; the earth opened her mouth, and swallowed up the flood the dragon had cast out of his mouth."

And the dragon was [angry] with the woman,
and went to make war with the remnant of her
seed, which keep the commandments of God,
and have the testimony of Jesus Christ.

—Verse 17

All of this started with my reading the Beatitudes, found in the book of Matthew, I began to think about the comparison of the attitudes Jesus had shared with His disciples on that day with what took place at creation. In Genesis 1, the Spirit of God was moving over the earth. Two things came to mind as I compared this activity with the events of Matthew 5. As the Spirit of God hovered over the destruction that had taken place on the earth after the fall of Lucifer and his followers, there must have been a time of mourning for God. The love of God is so encompassing of all situations, I can only imagine the grief that took place in His heart as He looked over the situation. Although Satan had devised evil in his heart and led a rebellion against God in heaven, the fallen angel had still been one of His creations, and he'd had a superior role in heaven. He had even been considered a "son of God," as were all the angels. It also came to my mind that everything God created has life, so the earth itself had to be in a state of shock and mourning, as well, because of the destruction that had taken place. How awesome it was for the earth to have been allowed to participate in the plan of salvation! The enemy thought he had destroyed God's plan before it could come to fruition, but God—as in all situations, because He is the Alpha and Omega, the beginning and the end, omniscient and omnipotent, all-knowing, and all-powerful—had calculated and revised the plan of salvation for victory to be won.

> *The earth mourneth and fadeth away, the world lanquisheth and fadeth away, the haughty people of the earth do languish.*
>
> **—Isaiah 24:4**

Here the prophet Isaiah was prophesying concerning the end times we are experiencing today. The world was also in this same state when God destroyed it with a flood during the time of Noah. The fallen angels, in another attempt to destroy God's plan of salvation, had crossed the line of God's order between the celestial realm and the earth, where humans lived. They had married the daughters of men and impregnated them; thus, giants were born into the earth.

Because of the evil influence of these rebellious angels, sin had now covered the earth. Romans 8:19 tells how the creation waits in eager expectation for the children of God to be revealed. So, all of creation is alive and waiting in expectancy for God's blessings, provision, and plan to come to fruition. God's love is so great that He sought to comfort both the earth and Himself. Recognizing the earth needed Him, the Creator—for without God, neither we, nor anything that was created by Him, can do anything—He began to move forward by creating a whole new world, but this time He added something even greater. He created man in His own image. He also devised a plan of salvation for mankind, for He saw the vulnerable state in which man could easily get himself through disobedience.

> *Blessed are the poor in spirit: for theirs is the kingdom of heaven. Blessed are they that mourn: for they shall be comforted.*
>
> **—Matthew 5:3–4**

What God did after this act of betrayal by Lucifer showed His heart, His mind, and His very character. His love was so great even during the chaos, rebellion, and confusion. Although He had to punish Satan and his followers, with a later judgment to follow at the appointed time, He yet extended Himself toward His creation and the plan He had devised before the foundation of the world.

As I continued to look at the creation account in Genesis 1, I saw where God began to separate light from darkness. Out of a chaotic situation came life and order, and God gave it purpose. The light was to continue to break the cycle of darkness, perpetually causing the day, and darkness was purposed to fall at the appointed time to create each night, a time for man to rest.

THE BE ATTITUDES

Let there be a firmament in the midst of the waters, and let it divide the waters from the waters . . .and it was so. And God called the firmament Heaven.

—Genesis 1:6–8

God continued to say, "Let there be . . ." until all of creation was made.

As I looked closer at the steps He took, I could see the connection of everything that was created. I could see how He created everything to communicate with each other in perfect harmony. Psalms 19:2–3 clarifies the symphony of the creation as it sings of God's glory, His praise, and His handiwork:

The heavens declare the glory of God; and the firmament sheweth his handywork. Day unto day uttereth speech, and night unto night sheweth knowledge. There is no speech nor language, where their voice is not heard.

No matter what language, nationality, creed, race, tribe, or species in all of creation, God has made Himself known. His greatness is displayed throughout the heavens and on the earth! The gathering of the waters under the heavens brought forth calibration and the restoration of the earth, and she renewed her strength. Sorrow and mourning had passed away, and newness of life began. As the earth yielded herself to the divine plan, at His command she began to birth the grass, trees yielding fruit, and seeds after their own kind. The circle of life was being renewed and restored. Once

BLESSINGS OF THE KINGDOM OF HEAVEN

again, the purpose of life was unfolding! What amazes me is how God, in His divine wisdom, calculated a purpose for every living thing that was created. He even calculated the timing and the seasons by which all things would operate, and He did this all in a six-day period, then reevaluated it and said, "Ah, it is good!"

While meditating on the greatness of God and His creation, I was drawn to watch a simple TV show on PBS simply called *Nature*. What I thought would be a time to watch a clean, wholesome show about different kinds of animals turned out to be an experience that went beyond my wildest dreams. I found myself watching for hours, even shedding tears of bewilderment and joy while experiencing the knowledge and wisdom of God in His mindset of creation.

The Holy Spirit took me on a journey, showing me just how vast God's wisdom and knowledge is. His tender mercy toward us, and His undying love for us, His creation, is beyond comparison to anything here on earth. He allowed me to see the depth of His provision and just how in tune He is with His creation. Some people think of Him as some giant, faraway God who sits on a huge throne way above the clouds, who looks down on us and every now and then graces us with His presence. This is not true! No, He is among His creatures every day, throughout the day, supplying needs, adjusting situations, shielding and protecting, and spreading His love day in and day out. Although everything was originally created during that six-day period, to this day it still perpetuates, calibrates, and calculates, just like a heavenly GPS reroutes our journey according to the destination, purpose, and plans God has for our lives—because there is no such thing called time with Him. He is the Alpha and Omega, the beginning and the end. He is omnipresent, yet He loves to spend time with us and love on us, His creation.

His understanding of everything He created reaches far beyond anything we could ever imagine. While watching the *Nature* program, I saw how every living thing has a divine, well-thought-out plan and purpose here on this beautiful earth. As I watched, I saw how God created us all to have our own unique instincts concerning life and how to survive on this earth. If we would only use our God-given gifts and talents, our natural abilities, to cope and navigate, tapping into our divine identity, purpose, and destiny, the inner portion of God in us would always lead us to victory. What looks like it will destroy you will actually cause life to spring forth from you!

For example, the forest protects itself, thriving on hurricanes and storms that produce lightning that starts fires—not to destroy, but to help the trees survive. The fires burn excess shrubs that would hinder the growth of the trees. The ash from the fires provides a certain type of nourishment. Along with the water from the rain and sun, the fires help new life to spring forth. God gives us beauty for ashes! This is God's way of providing what is needed to keep the forest alive and thriving.

The purpose of the forest is to provide shelter, or a habitat, for many of the creatures and animals that God created to live there. Everything in this world God made to depend on each other for survival. He appointed certain animals to eat certain things, such as the anteater, the plant and vegetation eaters, other certain animals and creatures to eat the dead things to keep the environment clean, and so on. The great whales only eat a particular fish. Each form of creation has its own designated form of survival. Everything has its place and purpose. God placed seeds within everything for reproduction, and thus the cycle, or circle, of life continues. Our earth is in a self-maintained system of rejuvenation and replenishment, demonstrating the awesome, incredible wonders of God! God is so intentional. Everything He made, as He said in Genesis 1, is good and has significance.

You should take some time to watch the Nature Channel. It will help you to understand God's creation and its purpose. You will be able to see the mind of God during the natural processes, understand His provision for everything that has been created, and experience His love and concern for us all. Nature shows us His character as a loving Father and as a tender nurturer. He is a protector and an awesome Creator of beauty. He is an artist extraordinaire!

How magnificent God is in His glory! When I saw the meticulous way He created each and every thing, even the color schemes and how it all was so unique and beautiful, I couldn't help but shed tears of amazement, bewilderment,

THE BE ATTITUDES

and joy all at the same time. And to think, He did it all for us to enjoy! Every morning I look to see the picture that He has painted in the sky in the form of a beautiful sunrise. Every day has been uniquely designed; never have I seen two sunrises just alike. Starting today, try to look out at the sky as often as you can to see what God has done. He is awesome!

After reading the Beatitudes in Matthew 5, I realized that Jesus decided to teach His disciples in person, as a father would teach his children, the attitudes that most exemplified the Kingdom of God as becoming His followers. Not only would it show forth the reactions of those who follow Him and His Kingdom, but it would prove to be a survival kit and a weapon against the enemy of their soul, Satan. These attitudes would ensure that no part of Satan and his evil ways would be found in them. The Word says in Revelation 12:9–10:

And the great dragon was cast out, that old serpent, called the Devil, and Satan, which deceiveth the whole world: he was cast out into the earth, and his angels were cast out with him. And I heard a loud voice saying in heaven, Now is come salvation, and strength, and the kingdom of our God, and the power of his Christ: for the accuser of our brethren is cast down, which accused them before our God day and night.

BLESSINGS OF THE KINGDOM OF HEAVEN

Satan is the accuser of the brethren. Because of his prideful nature and sinful ways, he was cast out of heaven. No longer would he participate in the worship and plans of God. Now *we* are the sons of God and the seed of righteousness, born of the Spirit in Christ, our Lord. The power transferred to Satan as a result of Adam and Eve's disobedience in the Garden of Eden was stripped from him by our Lord on the cross, and it has been transferred back to us as becoming saints. Satan's mission is now to destroy the Kingdom of God, and he goes forth throughout the earth seeking whom he can devour.

Having the attitude and mind of Christ is somewhat like our weapons of warfare, which are listed in Ephesians 6:10–18:

> *Finally, my brethren, be strong in the Lord, and in the power of his might. Put on the whole armour of God, that ye may be able to stand against the wiles of the devil. For we wrestle not against flesh and blood, but against the principalities, against powers, against the rulers of the darkness of this world, against spiritual wickedness in high places. Wherefore take unto you the whole armour of God, that ye may be able to withstand in the evil day, and having done all, to stand. Stand therefore, having your loins girt about with truth, and having on the breastplate of righteousness; and your feet shod with the preparation of the gospel of*

THE BE ATTITUDES

peace; Above all, taking the shield of faith, wherewith ye shall be able to quench all the fiery darts of the wicked. And take the helmet of salvation, and the sword of the Spirit, which is the word of God: Praying always with all prayer and supplication in the Spirit, and watching thereunto with all perseverance and supplication for all saints.

This is the very core of the Be Attitudes, which Jesus shared in Matthew 5. When the enemy comes in like a flood in our lives, we must stay in character, exemplifying the Kingdom of God. We must have the mind of Christ and allow the Spirit of God in us to lift a standard against him. God in us will cause us to triumph. When we remain in a position of love, forgiveness, and compassion toward our fellow man, this will conquer any evil that tries to hinder the plan of God in our lives. Let's go back to those definitions of the word *be*. We have seen that some of the meanings of the word *be* include "to exist or live," "to take place," "to happen," "to occur."

In the *Encyclopedia Britannica*, the word *be* is used to indicate the identity of a person or a thing, to describe the qualities of a person or thing, to indicate the condition of a person or thing, or to indicate the group, class, category, place, situation, or position of a person or thing. These definitions distinctly line up with the Beatitudes found in Matthew 5. We said we would look deeper into this later. Let's go with the Holy Spirit on this journey.

BLESSINGS OF THE KINGDOM OF HEAVEN

Matthew 5 begins just after Jesus was baptized by John, filled with the Holy Spirit, led into the wilderness to be tempted by Satan, and overcame the temptations by quoting the Word of God. He had set out on the mission His Father in heaven had ordained Him to fulfill. At the end of His discussion of the Beatitudes, Jesus said to His disciples, "Let your light so shine before men, that they may see your good works, and glorify your Father which is in heaven" (Matthew 5:16). His first stop was Capernaum, where He was to fulfill the prophecy found in the book of Isaiah: "The land of Zabulon, and the land of Nephthalim, by the way of the sea, beyond Jordan, Galilee of the Gentiles; the people which sat in darkness saw great light; and to them which sat in the region and shadow of death light is sprung up." It was like He was also fulfilling His own command of "Let there be light," but this time He was setting the example before men in the form of human flesh.

This Scripture also shows the importance of following the Holy Spirit into the destiny He has planned for each of our lives. Jesus started His journey by fulfilling God's plan for the Kingdom of God and for His Father's will to be manifested on the earth. He was indicating the identity of the Kingdom of God, the group from which He came, and His position of being the Son of God on the earth. By following the lead of the Holy Spirit, who had guided Him into this region to face temptation, divine connections were revealed, and He found His first ministry group.

Jesus was defining that word *be* in every detail as He

began His ministry. After He had chosen the Twelve who would become the governing body of His ministry after He returned to the Father after His resurrection, He began to demonstrate the power of the Kingdom of God here on earth. He went about healing all who were sick and diseased. Because of the miracles of healing and deliverance from demonic powers Jesus performed, a multitude followed Him in amazement, and many were eager to learn of this newfound Kingdom—for surely it was in a class and category they had never seen before.

The multitude had followed Jesus and His teachings for miles. Today He would tell them about the nature of the Kingdom of God and the blessings they would receive by following His example as He followed the Father's instruction, demonstrating the character of God, the will of God, and His Kingdom. Jesus began to teach them by allowing God's love to flow through Him, and He showed compassion for everyone who was afflicted by the enemy. He poured out the wisdom of the Holy Spirit and revealed the mysteries of heaven to the people, including how they could obtain the blessings of heaven by living a righteous life and following Him here on the earth.

Many times, the Sadducees and Pharisees lied about Him, tried to scandalize His name, and criticized Him. They even called him "Beelzebub," the name of a demonic spirit that they themselves operated under. Because of their own jealousy, they plotted together and attempted to kill Him. Jesus never allowed His rivals to provoke Him to move out of His divine character, the divine nature of His Father. He always exercised self-control, demonstrating the love of God and following His Father's will, even during trials and tribulation. He shared God's *agape* love, the unconditional love of the Father. The Word tells us in Romans 5:8: "But God commendeth his love toward us, in that, while we were yet sinners, Christ died for us." This is the attitude that a believer in Christ should have, or the state in which we should be as followers of Jesus, mirroring the divine nature of Christ here on earth. To allow the love of God to flow through us fluently, we must keep our hearts pure, our minds focused on the Kingdom of God, and our will yielded to the will of the Father and the plans He has for our lives. This requires prayer, or constant communication with Him. Sometimes this requires a time of fasting to empower our spirit man while decreasing the rule of our flesh.

In chapter 4, we saw that Jesus had fasted forty days and forty nights before entering His time of temptation. Because He was built up in communication through prayer, communication with His Father, He allowed His spirit man to access the necessary power from the Holy Spirit. Through fasting, while He denied His human flesh, He received direct words from heaven above, and all of this allowed Him to be led by the Spirit into His divine destiny, as He overcame the temptation to do evil from Satan. We, too, can overcome and gain the victory in our lives by following Jesus' example of denying Himself to be empowered by the Holy Spirit. This will allow us to

THE BE ATTITUDES

step into God's destiny and purpose for our lives. Not only will we be able to overcome in our own lives, but we will be able to lead others by example as Christ did, imparting the wisdom we have learned on our wilderness journey, as well as praying for the deliverance of others along the way. *Thank You, Jesus, for each nugget of experience that You have shared with us through Your Word, showing us the right way to salvation. You are the way, the truth, and the life, as You have said in Your Word. Continue to lead us and guide us in the way we should become as saints in Your Kingdom.*

> *Blessed are the poor in spirit for theirs is the kingdom of heaven.*
>
> **—Matthew 5:3**

Jesus demonstrated how to be poor in spirit by temporarily giving up His place in heaven and humbling Himself to the state of becoming human flesh called man to please the Father and to carry out the plan of salvation for all of mankind here on earth. Second Corinthians 8:9 tells us: "For ye know the grace of our Lord Jesus Christ, that, though he was rich, yet for your sakes he became poor, that ye through his poverty might be rich." Having the mind of Christ expedites our becoming like the Father and exemplifying the Kingdom of God here on earth. Philippians 2:5–8 states, "Let this mind be in you, which was also in Christ Jesus: Who, being in the form of God, thought it not robbery to be equal with God: But made

BLESSINGS OF THE KINGDOM OF HEAVEN

himself of no reputation, and took upon him the form of a servant, and was made in the likeness of men: and being found in fashion as a man, he humbled himself, and became obedient unto death, even the death of the cross."

Jesus has told us what the Kingdom of heaven is like. His nature is opposite of the prideful nature of Satan, who rebelled against his own Creator and tried to exalt himself to become equal to God. He coveted the position of the Creator, who made heaven and earth, and he craved the glory and honor that was given to him, as the angels in heaven worshiped him. The irony of it all is that Satan was the worship leader in heaven!

How often do we see this in churches? Because of the giftings and the anointing the Holy Spirit showers down on us, sometimes we crave the reverence of the people instead of giving all the honor and glory to our Savior. We tend to think it is our own greatness instead of God's goodness and His mercy that causes us not to be consumed. The worship of the God we serve becomes a performance to get accolades from men, rather than pointing them to Christ the Healer and Deliverer of our souls.

> *But the hour cometh, and now is, when the true worshippers shall worship the Father in spirit and in truth: for the Father seeketh such to worship him. God is a Spirit: and they that worship him must worship him in spirit and in truth.*
>
> **—John 4:23–24**

THE BE ATTITUDES

We must be ever so careful not to allow the spirit of Satan to overtake us with pride and blind us. Being led by the Holy Spirit, Jesus Himself was tempted by Satan in the wilderness after having fasted forty days and nights. Matthew 4:2–10 clearly points this out:

And when he had fasted forty days and forty nights, he was afterward a hungered. And when the tempter came to him, he said, if thou be the Son of God, command that these stones be made bread. But he answered and said, It is written, Man shall not live by bread alone, but by every word that proceedeth out of the mouth of God.

Here we can see Satan trying to entrap Jesus at His weakest moment. In the natural, He was weak because He hadn't eaten in such a long time, but in the Spirit, He was built up in the Word of God. The enemy also came after His self-image by saying, "If thou be the Son of God . . ." We must always know who we are in God, but most importantly, we must acknowledge that we are nothing without Him. Although He had the authority to command the stones to be made into bread, He knew that to overstep the authority of God, without having been given permission to do so, would have been equal to exalting His own agenda instead of exercising the will of the Father in His life. The worldly lust of the flesh is the number-one entrapment and danger zone to the soul of man.

The devil taketh him up into the holy city, and setteth him on a pinnacle of the temple, and saith unto him, If thou

BLESSINGS OF THE KINGDOM OF HEAVEN

be the Son of God, cast thyself down: for it is written, He shall give his angels charge concerning thee: and in their hands they shall bear thee up, lest at any time thou dash thy foot against a stone. Jesus said unto him, It is written again, Thou shalt not tempt the Lord thy God.

The enemy is so tricky and cunning. First, he appealed to the weakness of Jesus' flesh, but when He answered him with the Word of God, the devil came back with a twist in the application of the Word. We must be able to rightly divide the Word of truth. This is why it is so important to be filled and led by the Holy Spirit, for He will guide us into all truth (John 16:13). The devil also took Jesus up high on the pinnacle of the temple, representing position—the high and lofty place he himself had sought after when he was in heaven before he was cast down.

I think that where this temptation took place was very intentional. Here Satan is—at the Church! This was an attempt of the enemy to detour the purpose of Jesus, which was to reconcile man to God, and for His Bride, the Church, to be born. It is not about who we are, but it is about God's purpose and plan for our lives, which the enemy tries to steal. Once again, Jesus pointed out to the devil, it's only at God's command that we should move forward or jump into anything. Knowing that God has our back and fights for us as the Church is one thing, but trying to force His hand is something totally different. In all our ways, we should acknowledge Him, and He will direct our paths (Proverbs 3:6).

THE BE ATTITUDES

Again, the devil taketh him up into an exceeding high mountain, and sheweth him all the kingdoms of the world, and the glory of them; and saith unto him, All these things will I give thee, if thou wilt fall down and worship me. Then saith Jesus unto him, Get thee hence, Satan: for it is written, Thou shalt worship the Lord thy God, and him only shalt thou serve.

The lust of the eye and the pride of life—these are the biggest mistakes that Lucifer made while he was in heaven, trying to exalt himself above the throne of God and usurp His glory. God plainly states that He will share His glory with no one! Satan is the accuser of the brethren (Revelation 12:10); therefore, his goal is to kill, steal, and to destroy our relationship with God the Father, and His plan for all of creation—especially us, His children.

We are poor in spirit when we recognize our total spiritual destitution without Christ in our lives. Our total allegiance and dependence should be on God, for without Him we can do nothing. It is "in him [that] we live, and move, and have our being" (Acts 17:28). Our existence is in Him and Him only. Spiritual poverty occurs when someone is rich in material possessions, influence, and money, but is empty or bankrupt toward the things of God and His Kingdom. It is the difference between being poor in spirit and having spiritual poverty. Our attitude must always reflect the fact that without God, we can do nothing. It is He who enables us to gain wealth. It is His gifts and talents—and in many cases, His anointing—that causes us to excel.

BLESSINGS OF THE KINGDOM OF HEAVEN

All of creation depends on His provision, guidance, divine direction, and love. Acknowledging God as the Creator and the Sustainer of the universe is the state in which we, His creation, should reside. We should recognize that our entire existence is all part of His will and plan from the foundation of the world.

Blessed be the God and Father of our Lord Jesus Christ, who hath blessed us with all spiritual blessings in heavenly places in Christ: According as he hath chosen us in him before the foundation of the world, that we should be holy and without blame before him in love: Having predestinated us unto the adoption of children by Jesus Christ to himself, according to the good pleasure of his will.

—Ephesians 1:3–5

In whom also we have obtained an inheritance, being predestinated according to the purpose of him who worketh all things after the counsel of his own will.

—Verse 11

Being poor in spirit is not about how God views us, or even how other people view us; instead, it is in direct relation to how we view ourselves.

How art thou fallen from heaven. O Lucifer, son of the morning! how art thou cut down to the ground, which didst weaken the nations!

THE BE ATTITUDES

For thou hast said in thine heart, I will ascend into heaven, I will exalt my throne above the stars of God: I will sit also upon the mount of the congregation, in the sides of the north: I will ascend above the heights of the clouds; I will be like the most High.

—Isaiah 14:12–14

How foolish it is to think that creation could ever be above or equal to the Creator! We should always recognize and acknowledge that our complete dependence is on Him. Our hearts should always be humbled before Him. When I think of His grace and mercy toward us, my heart melts within me. How could such a loving, magnificent God love me so much that He would give His only begotten Son just for me? How could a loving Son humble Himself to such a degree and die just for me? His motivation was love to the highest degree.

Greater love hath no man than this, that a man lay down his life for his friends.

—John 15:13

His emancipating love caused Him to give His life so that we might become free.

In fact, under the Law almost everything is cleansed with blood, and without the shedding of blood there is no forgiveness [neither release from sin and its guilt, nor cancellation of the merited punishment].

—Hebrews 9:22 AMP

BLESSINGS OF THE KINGDOM OF HEAVEN

Without the shedding of blood, there is no redemption.

In Him we have redemption through His blood, the forgiveness of sins, according to the riches of His grace which He made to abound toward us in all wisdom and prudence.

—Ephesians 1:7–8 NKJV

God, help us to forever remain humble before You, always remembering the great sacrifice You made for the sins of the world.

And when he had given thanks, he brake it, and said, Take, eat; this is my body, which is broken for you: this do in remembrance of me. After the same manner also he took the cup, when he had supped, saying, this cup is the new testament in my blood: this do ye, as oft as ye drink it, in remembrance of me.

—1 Corinthians 11:24–25

To God be the glory forever. Amen!

2

Comforting Thoughts

Blessed are they that mourn:
for they shall be comforted.
—Matthew 5:4

The state of mourning is usually associated with a time of grief in our lives. Grieving is a process of healing after a time of death, tragedy, or loss. In times of grieving, we become vulnerable, without walls. Our hearts are melted within us. It is usually a time when we are at our lowest point in thought and mind. Feelings of depression and loneliness overtake our minds. Brokenness, shattered dreams, deferred hope, and the reality of loss break down barriers of callousness and stony places in our hearts. During this time, we are susceptible to repentance. It is a time when we reflect upon what we could have done better or what we did not do right. In these times, the darkness of the situation can easily send us into a state of despair.

THE BE ATTITUDES

God sees us in this state, and because He is a Father who cares, He is more present in our lives during these vulnerable moments:

> The eyes of the LORD are upon the righteous, and his ears are open unto their cry. . . . The righteous cry, and the LORD heareth, and delivereth them out of all their troubles. The LORD is nigh unto them that are of a broken heart; and saveth such as be of a contrite spirit.
>
> **—Psalm 37:15, 17–18**

God is more present in our lives at these times than ever before. He is there to shield us, to protect us, and to extend His mercy, grace, and love toward us. There is no better time to feel His love and comfort than when we are grieving. He is always near those who are broken and of a contrite spirit.

There are so many ways in which we can find ourselves in mourning. The most common is the death of a loved one. Especially when unexpected losses happen, they can throw us into a state of shock and even denial. It is so easy to think you will always have that person around, even when the Word lets us know that it is natural for death to occur. It's part of the circle of life. To die is just as normal as to be born. There is a divine appointment to bring us into this world, and there is also an appointment for us to leave this world.

COMFORTING THOUGHTS

The righteous perisheth, and no man layeth it to heart: and merciful men are taken away, none considering that the righteous is taken away from the evil to come. He shall enter into peace; they shall rest in their beds, each one walking in his uprightness.

—Isaiah 57:1–2

When we leave this earth, our appointment is to live forever with God, providing we have accepted Jesus as our Lord and Savior and strived to live a righteous life. Although accepting Him as our Lord and Savior qualifies us to enter heaven, repentance, or the willful turning away from our sins, shows our love and desire to rest in peace for eternity with Him.

It is appointed unto men once to die, but after this the judgment.

—Hebrews 9:27

Whether we accept Jesus or not, there is a divine appointment in heaven for us to stand before God and give an account of why we did or did not accept His plan of salvation—or Christ—into our lives.

Another form of mourning could be for the loss of a job. Often unforeseen circumstances occur in our lives, such as a loss of gainful employment. This can be frightening, even totally devastating to someone who is the head of the household and the breadwinner of the family. This type of mourning and grief can cause anxiety, uncertainty, fear,

THE BE ATTITUDES

and depression. This could very well be one of the darkest times in a person's life. During this time, the Holy Spirit is there, encouraging us to hold on. He reminds us of God's promise to supply all our needs according to His riches in glory by Christ Jesus (Philippians 4:19). He whispers hope into our hearts, giving us faith that everything is going to be alright.

In these dark times, we should always put our trust in God for He promises never to leave us or forsake us (Hebrews 13:5). Looking back on creation, we can see there is a provision of survival for everything that God created; how much more will He provide for those of us who were made in His own image?

Consider the lilies how they grow: they toil not, they spin not; and yet I say unto you, that Solomon in all his glory was not arrayed like one of these. If then God so clothe the grass, which is to day in the field, and to morrow is cast into the oven; how much more will he clothe you, O ye of little faith? And seek not ye what ye shall eat, or what ye shall drink, neither be ye of doubtful mind. For all these things do the nations of the world seek after; and your Father knoweth that ye have need of these things. But rather seek ye the kingdom of God; and all these things shall be added unto you.

—Luke 12:27–31

COMFORTING THOUGHTS

There are so many other things I could name that cause us to mourn: getting older and grieving the loss of activities to which we have been accustomed because of illness and disease in our bodies; broken marriages that causes us to mourn the loss of a relationship; or any other drastic change in our lives.

Our attitude in adverse situations should always be that of love, trust, and obedience to the Father, "knowing that the trying of [our] faith worketh patience. But let patience have her perfect work, that ye may be perfect and entire" (James 1:3–4). Here James is reminding us that although we go through these trials and tribulations, tears, inconveniences, and irritations in our lives, God is the ultimate completion of our purpose. He promises never to leave us nor forsake us. When we are weak, He is strong.

And he said unto me, My grace is sufficient for thee: for my strength is made perfect in weakness. Most gladly therefore will I rather glory in my infirmities, that the power of Christ may rest upon me. Therefore I take pleasure in infirmities, in reproaches, in necessities, in persecutions, in distresses for Christ's sake: for when I am weak, then am I strong.

—2 Corinthians 12:8–10

Life happens, but our stance in life must be to have the attitude that God is in control over every situation that comes into our lives. We are to be in the mindset of knowing

THE BE ATTITUDES

that God is with us, and He is a Father who cares for us. We cannot manage situations that come in our lives alone, but knowing that He is a God of comfort, we can rest in Him.

> *O bless our God, ye people, and make the voice of his praise to be heard: Which holdeth our soul in life, and suffereth not our feet to be moved.*

—Psalm 66:8–9

Not only does mourning happen when natural disasters take place, but our spirit man cries out to God when we are found in a destitute place in God. Because Jesus was teaching the Beatitudes of life, I believe it was mostly this type of mourning to which He was referring: the mourning of our souls being lost. This type of mourning was in direct correlation to our being poor in spirit. When we recognize our sinful state as it relates to the holiness of God, we mourn because of the helplessness we feel, caught in the bondage of sin.

If we draw near to God, He will draw near to us (James 4:8). We must commit our ways to the Lord, willfully submitting ourselves to God for the cleansing of all unrighteousness, confessing our sins and admitting we cannot live holy lives without Him. We should pursue God with everything in us, acknowledging it is the shed blood of Christ that cleanses us from all unrighteousness.

Sin can cause us to turn a blind eye and have deaf ears when the Holy Spirit tries to show us the way. When He

COMFORTING THOUGHTS

whispers in our ear, reproving us of our sins and iniquities, we push past the red flags and continue on our own way. We point the finger at others and their shortcomings, but we never acknowledge the wrong in our own lives.

Thank God for His mercy and grace, as well as the fact that the Holy Spirit never gives up on us. He continues to try to convict us of our sins—not to harm us, but so that salvation, healing, and the deliverance of our souls would come. When we mourn the state of our souls, recognizing that we need Jesus to deliver us from the evil within, this type of mourning brings the presence of God, healing, and deliverance into our lives.

When we die to the lust of the eye, the lust of the flesh, and the pride of life, all of heaven rejoices.

> *Precious in the sight of the LORD is the death of his saints. O LORD, truly I am thy servant; I am thy servant, and the son of thine handmaid: thou hast loosed my bonds.*
> **—Psalm 116:15–16**

> *Likewise, I say unto you, there is joy in the presence of the angels of God over one sinner that repenteth.*
> **—Luke 15:10**

The Holy Spirit is always there to lead us and guide us into all righteousness, and to comfort us in our times of mourning.

THE BE ATTITUDES

Like as a father pitieth his children, so the LORD pitieth them that fear him. For he knoweth our frame; he remembereth that we are dust.

—Psalm 103:13–14

We should always have the attitude or be of the awareness that God is our help. He is our shield. He is everything we need. We should always seek His guidance in prayer, accepting His love and care for us.

Casting all your care upon him; for he careth for you.

—1 Peter 5:7

3

The Inheritance of the Meek

Blessed are the meek:
for they shall inherit the earth.
—Matthew 5:5

Meekness is essentially an attitude or quality of heart whereby a person is willing to accept and submit without resistance to the will and desire of someone else, particularly, in this case, God.

Spiritual meekness is an imperative virtue for Christian leaders. Not only does it involve submitting our wills to God, but it also means standing up and speaking out against immorality and injustice to others. One example of this kind of meekness would be Moses.

According to the Word, Moses was one of the meekest men on earth, yet he stood against Pharaoh and the harsh treatment of the Israelites. When his sister, Miriam, and his brother, Aaron, spoke against him because of their jealousy and envy, he prayed for them, that God would refrain from His judgment on them.

In the wilderness, after coming down from Mount Sinai with the tablets of the Law in his hands, Moses found his followers worshiping false idols, he immediately reacted by throwing the tablets down and reprimanding the people.

My thoughts about this took me to one of today's meek leaders. Martin Luther King Jr. was one who displayed meekness. During desperation, injustice, inhumane, and immoral acts toward God's people, he stood up for justice in a profound, peaceful, but powerful way. He chose to stand for righteousness and the mission that God ordained him to do, even in the face of death.

Meekness sometimes can be confused with being weak, soft, or a pushover, but it is just the opposite. Meekness is an inner strength that is exercised by choice. It means having the ability to restrain from seeking your own will, but rather give into the needs or will of others and their agenda. I believe this directly coincides with the virtues of being poor in spirit and mourning one's need for the fulfillment of God's purpose in their lives.

Meekness is one of the characteristics of God, and a virtue of the Holy Spirit. Being meek helps to tame the

THE INHERITANCE OF THE MEEK

unruliness of the soul, as we yield to the nature of Christ in us. It has been said by some that meekness is strong, not weak; active, not passive; courageous, not timid; restrained, not excessive; modest, not self-aggrandizing; and gracious, not brash.

Meekness is also said to be the quality of those who are God-fearing, righteous, humble, teachable, and patient under suffering. Those who possess this attribute are willing to follow Jesus Christ, and their temperament is calm, docile, tolerant, and submissive.

When considering the fruit of the Spirit listed in Galatians, we see that some of these very attributes of the Spirit are found.

> *But the fruit of the Spirit is love, joy, peace, longsuffering, gentleness, goodness, faith, meekness, temperance: against such there is no law.*
>
> **—Galatians 5:22–23**

Meekness is translated from the Greek word *praus*, which is translated as "strength under control" and "willing to submit." There is a difference between being in submission to and conforming to the ways of others. To conform means to act in accordance with expectations; to behave in the manner of others, especially because of social pressure. As pertaining to being a follower of Christ, we must not be conformed to this worldly system, but be transformed by the renewing of our minds (Romans 12:2).

55

THE BE ATTITUDES

*If any man be in Christ, he is a new creature:
old things are passed away; behold, all things
are become new.*

—2 Corinthians 5:17

Receiving Christ into our lives and confessing Him as Lord and Savior transforms us from the system of this world into the Kingdom of God. Although we are in this world and no longer of this world, our allegiance and will must be submitted to Christ. We must now walk circumspectly, as children of Christ and not conforming to this world. There must be a line of demarcation between the two—the world and the Kingdom of God.

When confronted with the worldly system of man and the things of God, Jesus spoke boldly and taught His disciples to render unto Caesar the things that are Caesar's and unto God the things that are God's (Mark 12:17). Here Jesus was saying that because we live in this world, we must obey the law of the land, but because we are submitted to the will of God, we must abide by His Word, which represents the governing Kingdom of God. It must take precedence over anything else. Walking in meekness can be challenging at times, but a regimen of prayer and occasional fasting will help to keep our flesh under subjection to the will of God. Feeding the spirit man with the Word of God will help to sustain us when we are under attack by the enemy.

We said the Greek word for *meekness* is *praus*, translated as "strength under control." Without submission to the Holy

THE INHERITANCE OF THE MEEK

Spirit, we can easily be provoked. We are to be strong and powerful, walking under the anointing of the Holy Spirit, yet willing to submit to His will, having control of our soulish realm, particularly our emotions. When we represent Christ as our Lord and Savior, it should be in a way that our behavior among others always reflects His character.

Let your light so shine before men, that they may see your good works, and glorify your Father which is in heaven.

—Matthew 5:16

Our lives should always mirror and reflect Christ. Our aim should be to create a lifestyle that makes people think about the value of having God in their lives.

Ye are our epistle written in our hearts, known and read of all men: Forasmuch as ye are manifestly declared to be the epistle of Christ ministered by us, written not with ink, but with the Spirit of the living God; not in tables of stone, but in fleshly tables of the heart.

—2 Corinthians 3:2–3

We are living epistles. A person will watch and read our lives before they ever will pick up a Bible. Having meekness as a virtue could surely lead someone to Christ.

Meekness is a very beautiful thing, although sometimes it can be painful.

> *Cease from anger, and forsake wrath: fret not thyself in any wise to do evil. For evildoers shall be cut off: but those that wait upon the LORD, they shall inherit the earth.*
>
> **—Psalm 37:8–9**

Praus indicates a decided strength of disciplined calmness. It is a virtue that exemplifies the willingness to share and sacrifice on behalf of others. This is the whole picture of what Jesus did for us. The Beatitudes were a step-by-step rehearsal of what was about to happen in the life of Christ. He was preparing His disciples for the ministry and mission that He Himself was about to fulfill. He led by example. Teaching them ahead of time prepared them for the encounters they would have on the journey with Him, as well as after He returned to the father. Actions speak louder than words, so as He went on His journey, because of His teachings, they were able to monitor His actions as He was confronted by his adversaries. Not only were the disciples present, but there were thousands of people there, listening and observing His actions as the Pharisees and Sadducees challenged and threatened Him.

This will also happen in our lives when we profess Christ and take a stand for Him. Many of televangelists go through this same scrutiny on a large scale because of their walk with Christ. Whether we have a large audience or small, we should always think before reacting, *WWJD*, or, What would Jesus do in this situation? This is the question we should ask ourselves.

THE INHERITANCE OF THE MEEK

No matter what the Sadducees and Pharisees did to Jesus, He never aborted the mission God had given to Him or allowed them to distract Him from His ministry here on earth. He was meek and lowly in heart, but He stood on the authority of who He was in God, and who God was in Him. He was always searching for those who needed healing and deliverance. And today, He is always gentle, kind, and tender toward us, full of compassion. Whereas meekness is a type of humility, it is geared more toward having self-control and long-suffering toward others, love and gentleness toward each other. Meekness is a condition of the heart. When we find ourselves losing our self-control, it is usually because our heart is either in a state of unforgiveness or engulfed by bitterness. Because we have been offended or hurt by someone, or a loss has occurred in our lives, we lash out in anger. If we bottled up these emotions, they would show up in our love walk.

This is the character that Jesus portrayed while on earth. His whole passion was to glorify the Father and to finish His work. Even when He was crucified, He looked up to heaven with love and said, "Father, forgive them; for they know not what they do" (Luke 23:34). This was the ultimate demonstration of His character, the ultimate show of meekness!

4

Filled to the Brim

Blessed are they which do hunger and thirst after righteousness: for they shall be filled.

—Matthew 5:6

When I think of this Scripture, I am reminded of two things. First, I think of Jesus, when He said, "I am the bread of life: he that cometh to me shall never hunger; and he that believeth on me shall never thirst" (John 6:35). The Semitic origin of the word *gava* is "to hunger or "to be empty," "to have a longing to be filled with something." In this verse of Scripture, Jesus was alluding to spiritual hunger. Spiritual hunger is feeling deprived of a sense of purpose, passion, pleasure, or joy in one's life. This blessing of being filled comes with having a personal, unquenching desire to know God, to the extent that it causes us to pursue Him. This hunger comes from having a void in our lives, along with an inner knowing in the depths of our soul that the only thing that can fill it is God.

THE BE ATTITUDES

Although, by nature, we were born in sin and shaped in iniquity, the DNA that lies within us came about when God breathed into Adam the breath of life, and man became a living soul. That "be" part of him, which was locked into his soul, was the part of God that every man longs for. It's like knowing we are a part of something higher and greater than life itself.

Like an orphan who pursues the destiny of finding his or her true birth parents, we long for the true knowledge of who God is and who we are in Him. Through the fall of Adam and Eve, who were made in God's own image and likeness, because of their disobedience and sin, our identity became hidden. We became orphans. Because we were shaped in iniquity and sin, Satan became our foster parent. The separation between man and his Creator caused a distortion between the image in which we were created and the way of life that the enemy of our souls shaped for us.

We began to portray the character of Satan and the ways of the world system, which we were taught by our foster parent, Satan. God, in His wisdom, created a default coding system in us where our identity would never be lost, somewhat like the way we program computers. Man was created in God's own image as a triune being. As the Father, Son, and Holy Spirit are one, we were created body, soul, and spirit—as one, united human being.

FILLED TO THE BRIM

For there are three that bear record in heaven, the Father, the Word, and the Holy Ghost: and these three are one.

—1 John 5:7

And the LORD God formed man of the dust of the ground, and breathed into his nostrils the breath of life; and man became a living soul,

—Genesis 2:7

When God breathed into man's nostrils, He released a part of Himself, and we *be–came*! Because God is a Spirit, the spirit part of man became our DNA—the identity or essence of who we are. God formed a body of the dust of the ground, breathed a portion of His Spirit into the body, and the word *be* caused us to exist in His image. The Word says, "man became," because the word *came* is the past tense of *come*, so he wasn't *coming*; God already existed. He shared a portion of who He is with us. The part of us that became a living soul is the nature of God in us, the ability to think, decide, and love. It includes our mind or intellect, our will, and our emotions.

And the very God of peace sanctify you wholly; and I pray God your whole spirit and soul and body be preserved blameless unto the coming of our Lord Jesus Christ.

—1 Thessalonians 5:23

THE BE ATTITUDES

We live from our connection with God; our spirit is one with God. As we cannot separate who we are from our parents, neither can we separate who we are from God. That internal connection gives us an eternal connection that cannot be seen or broken.

> *So we fix our eyes not on what is seen, but on what is unseen, since what is seen is temporary, but what is unseen is eternal.*
>
> **—2 Corinthians 4:18**

> *God that made the world and all things therein, seeing that he is Lord of heaven and the earth, dwelleth not in temples made with hands; neither is worshipped with men's hands, as though he needed any thing, seeing he giveth to all life, and breath, and all things; and hath made of one blood all nations of men for to dwell on all the face of the earth, and hath determined the times before appointed, and bounds of their habitation; That they should seek the Lord, if haply they might feel after him, and find him, though he be not far from every one of us: For in him we live, and move, and have our being; as certain also of your own poets have said, For we are also his offspring.*
>
> **—Acts 17:24–28**

Part of man—his spirit—can experience perfect fellowship with God. Deep within us, our spirits began to cry out to Abba Father, seeking a place of rest. If physical hunger is a set of feelings that leads people to search for food, then spiritual hunger is a set of experiences and longings that compel us to search for God. Just as our body needs food to survive, our spirit needs God to thrive. A divine hunger drives us to find out more about God.

Because God loves us so much, and because He knows our thoughts, our hearts' cry, the very core of us, He sent His Son, Jesus, to die on the cross to cleanse us from all unrighteousness and redeem us from the enemy and sin. When Jesus came to free us from our sins, He became the righteousness that was missing in our lives. When we hunger and thirst for righteousness, or we pursue Him and the Kingdom of God, He then reaches out and delivers us from the evil influence of Satan. When we believe on Him and the work of the cross that cleanses us from our sins, then we are filled with righteousness, because of the shed blood of Christ. Thank You, Jesus! Glory to God!

Hunger for God is the longing to encounter Him, to be with Him, and to be filled with His Spirit. When we are hungry for God and His Presence, we will do whatever it takes to get close to Him. When we worship God with all our heart, He, in return, will grace us with His Presence. The place of intimacy is where we will not only catch the revelation He wants to give us, but also capture His heart.

Draw near to God, and he will draw near to you. Cleanse your hands, you sinners, and purify your hearts, you double-minded.

—James 4:8 ESV

When we place our focus on the things of God, recognize our sinful state, and are willing to give up our former lifestyle, true repentance opens the door of our hearts and invites the righteousness of Christ to come in. The condition of the heart becomes pure at this moment, and conception of the new birth can take place. It is the condition of the heart and the laying down of our own will, as Christ laid down His own life, that brings forth fulfillment. It is the ultimate ecstasy in life that one can receive!

> *Behold, I stand at the door, and knock: if any man hear my voice, and open the door, I will come in to him, and will sup with him, and he with me.*

—Revelation 3:20

Having a healthy appetite for the Word of God is crucial for a productive life in Christ. In the natural world, it is wonderful to receive a cool, refreshing drink of lemonade, tea, or whatever we are craving to quench our thirst. We can drink a gallon of our favorite beverage, but in the end, only a cool drink of water will completely satisfy the body. So it is in the Spirit: Only a cool drink of the Word of God can satisfy the longing, the thirst in our souls, for God. Just like the manna that came down from heaven to feed the children of Israel was both spiritual and fulfilling, so is the Word of God to us. According to Exodus 16, God fed His people angels' food for forty years.

FILLED TO THE BRIM

As the hart panteth after the water brooks, so panteth my soul after thee, O God. My soul thirsteth for God, for the living God: when shall I come and appear before God?

—Psalm 42:1

There is a thirst that only God can fulfill in your life. This thirst draws from a well of living water that overflows into your life and pours out blessings. This is where the divine meets the supernatural in our lives and gives encounters and revelation knowledge that's never been known to man.

I am reminded of the story of the Samaritan woman in John 4. She encountered Jesus at the well, and He gave her living water. He said to her:

If thou knewest the gift of God, and who it is that saith unto thee, Give me to drink; thou wouldest have asked of him, and he would have given thee living water.

—Verse 10

Whosoever drinketh of this water shall thirst again; But whosoever drinketh of the water that I shall give him shall never thirst; but the water that I shall give him shall be in him a well of water springing up into everlasting life.

—verses 13–14

Jesus gave her an eternal word of supernatural provision for her soul; so it is when we read the Word of God.

> *It is the spirit that quickeneth; the flesh profiteth nothing: the words that I speak unto you, they are spirit, and they are life.*
>
> **—John 6:63**

We must always have a hunger and thirst for God's Word, for it is our lifeline to salvation. His Word is living in His Presence, which brings the fullness of joy; without it, we would perish. We must stay connected to the eternal to flourish. The Word is also what washes and cleanses us. It gives us direction and teaches us how to live a godly life, how to fulfill that hunger and thirst for righteousness.

> *I am the true vine, and my Father is the husbandman. . . . Abide in me, and I in you. As the branch cannot bear fruit of itself, except it abide in the vine; no more can ye, except ye abide in me. Without me ye can do nothing. . . . If ye abide in me, and my words abide in you, ye shall ask what ye will, and it shall be done unto you.*
>
> **—John 15:1, 4–5, 7**

This is the divine connection.

Coinciding with the previous Beatitudes—blessings on the poor in spirit, the mournful, and the meek—to hunger and thirst after righteousness means you are in a state in life where you want to live a godly life. It also means you

FILLED TO THE BRIM

are ready to commit to a lifestyle of reading and searching God's Word to learn how He would want you to live.

Congratulations! You are in a state where nothing will quench your thirst or fulfill your heart's desire except knowing more of Him.

Give us this day our daily bread.

—Matthew 6:11

Father, as we open our hearts to You, we pray that You will fill us to the brim and even overflowing with Your Presence.

As the hart panteth after the water brooks, so panteth my soul after thee, O God. My soul thirsteth for God, for the living God: when shall I come and appear before God?

—Psalm 42:1–2

These verses are the sentiments of our heart. Fill us with Your presence, Your Holy Spirit, Your total essence, until we cannot contain any more. We hunger and thirst after righteousness, so that we may be vessels of honor, carrying Your glory throughout the earth to share with others, in Jesus' name. Amen.

5

Unlimited Mercy

Blessed are the merciful:
for they shall obtain mercy.
—Matthew 5:7

What is *mercy*? According to Encyclopedia.com, *mercy* is "compassion or forgiveness shown toward someone whom it is within one's power to punish or harm." It is also "forgiveness or withholding punishment." It can be characterized as "relieving someone's pain." Having mercy is equal to "benevolence, kindness, and pity for one toward another." Mercy is a divine characteristic of God, that, when demonstrated through one's life benefits, both the man who shows mercy and the man who receives it is blessed. Mercy is a blessing of God's love flowing freely through man to others here on earth. It takes a supple heart to show true acts of mercy. This kind of heart is pliable, willing for God to use for His purpose in the earth.

THE BE ATTITUDES

For the eyes of the Lord run to and fro throughout the whole earth, to shew himself strong in the behalf of them whose heart is perfect toward him.

—2 Chronicles 16:9

We are to always imitate God in His mercifulness:

Be ye therefore merciful, as your Father also is merciful.

—Luke 6:36

Being merciful to others is serving God and ministering to His needs. We should look through the eyes of the Holy Spirit to see the needs of others and be willing to sacrifice for them, as Christ did for us. Instead of being judgmental, we should search out what the need is and actively relieve the pain or burden by meeting that person's need.

What doth it profit, my brethren, though a man say he hath faith, and have not works? Can faith save him? If a brother or sister be naked, and destitute of daily food, and one of you say unto them, Depart in peace, be ye warmed and filled; notwithstanding ye give them not those things which are needful to the body; what doth it profit?

—James 2:14–16

UNLIMITED MERCY

There is a reward for performing such acts of kindness:

> *Then shall the King say unto them on his right hand, Come, ye blessed of my Father, inherit the kingdom prepared for you from the foundation of the world: For I was an hungred, and ye gave me meat: I was thirsty, and ye gave me drink: I was a stranger, and ye took me in: Naked, and ye clothed me: I was sick, and ye visited me: I was in prison, and ye came unto me. Then shall the righteous answer him, saying, Lord, when saw we thee an hungred, and fed thee? or thirsty, and gave thee drink? When saw we thee a stranger, and took thee in? or naked, and clothed thee? Or when saw we thee sick, or in prison, and came unto thee? And the King shall answer and say unto them, Verily I say unto you, inasmuch as ye have done it unto one of the least of these my brethren, ye have done it unto me.*

—Matthew 25:34–40

God shows mercy to us daily. What we might deem as a narrow escape coming from a near-death experience, or a breakthrough in our finances, the stock market falling just right, even in times of destitution, being homeless, it is God's mercy during these times that we are not consumed. Sometimes we are in direct rebellion against God's will for our lives, and we know it, yet He still extends His love and mercy toward us. Who wouldn't serve a God like that!

THE BE ATTITUDES

In the height of his rebellion, Jonah did just the opposite of what he knew God had called him to do—just because he didn't think it was right for God to extend His mercy toward the people of Nineveh. As if he had a patent on the mercies of God! How many times have we been judgmental instead of merciful? God has a way of bringing out the best in us. Jonah found himself swallowed by a great fish! He soon repented, but God, during his rebellion, extended His mercy and did not allow the huge fish to kill him. Neither did Jonah drown while he was in the fish's belly. God eventually caused the fish to spew him out onto land, and Jonah finished the work he was called to do. And his efforts brought repentance and deliverance for that whole city of people. What a tragedy it would have been if Jonah had not obeyed the Lord!

After Jonah had finished his mission, however, he still had not seen the error of his judgmental ways. He went out into a field and sat down. Then:

> *He prayed unto the LORD, and said, I pray thee, O LORD, was not this my saying, when I was yet in my country? Therefore I fled before unto Tarshish: for I knew that thou art a gracious God, and merciful, slow to anger, and of great kindness, and repentest thee of the evil.*
>
> **—Jonah 4:1–2**

God had pity on him, even in the midst of his self-righteous ways, and He caused a plant to grow to cover him with shade from the sun. God covers us even when we stray from His plans for our lives. Thank You, Jesus! (This story can be found in Jonah 1 through 4, for your extensive reading.)

When we see others who are destitute—such as the homeless, drug addicted, wayward children committing senseless crimes—we should not be so quick to judge, but rather we should be willing to help and find a solution to the problem. Clearly there are some deep, underlying issues they are facing. Reaching out to give them a hand up, not a handout, shows God's mercy and love.

When others experience God's love through us, it rekindles hope that has been lost. It will show the wayward children that there is Someone who cares about them, and that God has not forsaken them in their time of trouble. Mercy extended is God's love touching others' lives and causing change. Let us be that agent of change in our communities, in our neighbors' lives, and in this next generation.

The warmth we feel when we help others is the love of God being reciprocated back to us, supplying us with what is needed in our lives. When you find a truly merciful man, you will find a whole man—nothing missing, nothing lacking according to God's standards. It is then that we are more like Christ, mirroring the image that He portrayed while on earth.

THE BE ATTITUDES

They that are whole have no need of the physician, but they that are sick: I came not to call the righteous, but sinners to repentance.

—Mark 2:17

How God anointed Jesus of Nazareth with the Holy Ghost and with power: who went about doing good, healing all that were oppressed of the devil; for God was with him.

—Acts 10:38

Go ye into all the world, and preach the gospel to every creature, He that believeth and is baptized shall be saved; but he that believeth not shall be damned. And these signs shall follow them that believe; In my name shall they cast out devils; they shall speak with new tongues; they shall take up serpents; and if they drink any deadly thing, it shall not hurt them; they shall lay hands on the sick, and they shall recover.

—Mark 16:15–18

This is who He is. This is who we are!

As we have the ability to speak a word in season that will uplift a soul, to lay hands on the sick through the power of the Holy Spirit and have them be healed, or to just go into the kitchen and cook a meal to serve to the needy—whatever the capacity in which we are God's hands, His heart, His mercy—let us do it with all diligence. Let us be love and show compassion one toward the other, remembering the passion of Christ that He showed toward us!

Heavenly Father, rekindle the love and compassion in our hearts and cause us to fall in love with mercy once again. Let the tenderness of Your heart permeate ours that we might share the love of God with others. As You have shown us Your tender mercies, peel back the callousness of our hearts that we may feel once again and be the vessels You have called us to be in these last days. In a world where the love of many has waxed cold, Holy Spirit, light a fire down in our souls that others may see and come to be healed and delivered, in Jesus' name! Amen.

There is one more mercy that is burning in my soul—the mercy of forgiveness. When we forgive others for their trespasses against us, the debts we feel are owed to us, the punishment we feel they deserve, our heavenly Father also forgives us and delivers us from unrighteousness. Not only are we released from the dreadfulness and burden of unforgiveness, which can easily turn into anger, bitterness, hatred, strife, betrayal, and even murder in our hearts, but that person is released from the cords that we unknowingly bind them with, as well.

Remember, all things are both natural and spiritual. Our thought process is a direct channel that can either open demonic portals, which will allow the infiltration of evil strongholds to enter our hearts or souls, or bring about righteousness, which produces love, forgiveness,

THE BE ATTITUDES

and compassion. This is why the enemy attacks our minds with evil visions of the betrayal or offenses others have committed in our lives. Although to us we are "just rethinking the situation," he knows that if he deceives us into dwelling on it long enough, it will cause vain imaginations of revenge, ill will toward that person or persons, or even thoughts of committing crimes such as vandalism, assaults, or even murder. May I remind you that to gossip, to speak lies about someone, to scandalize purposely, or to falsely besmirch someone's name is to destroy or murder that person's character.

Unforgiveness is a strongman, or a demonic spirit, that can open a channel in our lives for other demonic spirits, called strongholds, to enter. Many who are sick and diseased have unforgiveness as the root cause. Undetected causes of maladies in someone's life can almost always be traced back to unforgiveness. As we allow these vain imaginations to continue to dwell in us, they will eventually enter our hearts. We will begin to show signs of anger, bitterness, and all the other emotions we mentioned above. We tend to rehash the story to others, while bashing the character of the one who brought the offense or betrayal against us. This is a type of "murder" we rarely think about. When we are speaking ill toward others, we are destroying, or "murdering," that person's character. Have you ever seen or heard someone who is filled with unforgiveness say, "I hope they drop dead"? The power of life and death are in the tongue.

Death and life are in the power of the tongue:
and they that love it shall eat the fruit thereof.

—Proverbs 18:21

Releasing these types of words against another person's life gives permission for the forces of darkness to try to bring it to pass. It also can send cords that will bind up in the spirit realm every dream, venture, and future hope of that person. This is a form of witchcraft, of which we are usually totally oblivious. How the enemy subtly deceives us in moments of weakness and uses us against one another!

Casting down vain imaginations is a spiritual weapon that we must use to be victorious, overcomers of unforgiveness.

> *For the weapons of our warfare are not carnal, but mighty through God to the pulling down of strongholds; casting down imaginations, and every high thing that exalted itself against the knowledge of God, and bringing into captivity every thought to the obedience of Christ.*

—2 Corinthians 10:4–5

Confessing our faults and thoughts of unforgiveness helps us to expose the enemy's attack against us and solicits help from others to pray for us so that God would intervene and help us.

THE BE ATTITUDES

Confess your faults one to another, and pray one for another, that ye may be healed. The effectual fervent prayer of a righteous man availeth much.

—James 5:16

Showing mercy guards our heart from callousness and unrighteousness. Love conquers all! Love sets in motion a pureness that comes straight from the Father by the Holy Spirit. It purifies the mind, heart, and soul. It causes us to show compassion for the needs of others and helps us to pray for them.

And above all things have fervent charity among yourselves: for charity shall cover the multitude of sins.

—1 Peter 4:8 KJV

And above all things have fervent love for one another, for "love will cover a multitude of sins."

—1 Peter 4:8 NKJV

Let the words of my mouth, and the meditation of my heart, be acceptable in thy sight, O LORD, my strength, and my redeemer.

—Psalm 19:14

6

Pure Eyesight

Blessed are the pure in heart:
for they shall see God.
—Matthew 5:8

There was a reason why Jesus told His disciples to forgive "seventy times seven" in Matthew 18:22. To forgive so many times keeps our heart and motives pure in the sight of God, our Father. It also keeps us humble, walking in love. God is love; therefore, when we choose love over unforgiveness, there is an immediate response from heaven: the Holy Spirit shares the love of God within our hearts, which supersedes all unrighteousness. *Agape* love permeates our being, and we find ourselves ministering the love of God as we pray for one another.

Hope maketh not ashamed; because the love
of God is shed abroad in our hearts by the
Holy Ghost which is given unto us.
—Romans 5:5

It amazes me how certain Scriptures line up in number, as the meaning of that number. For example, this verse is found in Romans 5:5, and the number five represents grace: God's unmerited, undeserved favor, or His love. Christ demonstrated this pure love when He laid down His life for us. We did nothing to earn this love, but it was shown toward us without repentance. God had mercy on us, seeing we needed a Savior. Having pureness of heart causes us to do the same to others, to look beyond their faults and to see their needs. Is it an easy task? No, but it's not of ourselves. When we make the choice to do so, this is what sets in motion that pure love that covers a multitude of sins.

Being pure in heart saturates the soul. It causes the soul to live, thrive, and have communication with the Holy Spirit that brings forth revelation of the Kingdom of heaven like never before. Divine inspiration and saturation of the anointing can flow freely, without blockage or hinderances. When our hearts are not pure, we become stagnated, clogged up like a hardened artery or a blocked drain. It stops the flow of the Holy Spirit in our lives. We are unable to properly function and move into our future. It causes us to be stuck in our past. The movement of the Holy Spirit is always forward and in a progression. When you have a chance, go to a river, lake, or ocean—whatever you can— and watch the flowing of the water. It renews itself with freshness by this process. For our spirit to stay refreshed and renewed, we must guard our hearts.

PURE EYESIGHT

Keep thy heart with all diligence; for out of it are the issues of life.

—Proverbs 4:23

Raw emotions unchecked can ruin relationships with both God and man.

But your iniquities have separated between you and your God, and your sins have hid his face from you, that he will not hear.

—Isaiah 59:2

Let us be aware of the wiles of the enemy and remain pure in heart and mind. We are all in this together, having a common enemy: not each other, but the devil.

When I think of pureness, I think of the transparency of water. Another way to keep a pure heart is to have transparency in our emotions and thoughts before God. If we find ourselves in situations that could easily provoke us to close our hearts off to others, it not only puts a barrier between us, but it also causes that clog we talked about earlier. It can cause an effect like a dam in the river. There is water on both sides, but neither can get to the other. The water on both sides may cause some things to grow, but right where the dam meets, there is dead, or still, water. You may find yourself moving, but there is always that weight you feel tugging, holding you back. If that is the case for you, call out to God for deliverance. He can only get glory out of our lives when we are exemplifying love.

THE BE ATTITUDES

By this shall all men know that ye are my disciples, if ye have love one to another.

—John 13:35

Right motives cause right relationships. The blessing in forgiveness is a pure heart that pours life into others.

Then said he unto me, These waters issue out toward the east country, and go down into the desert, and go into the sea: which being brought forth into the sea, the waters shall be healed. And it shall come to pass, that every thing that liveth, which moveth, whithersoever the rivers shall come, shall live: and there shall be a very great multitude of fish, because these waters shall come thither: for they shall be healed; and every thing shall live whither the river cometh.

—Ezekiel 47:8–9

Jesus told His disciples, "I will make you fishers of men." In comparison, the love that flows freely without taint brings forth healing to those it touches. We are that stream of water, or that river of life, to others.

He that believeth on me, as the scripture hath said, out of his belly shall flow rivers of living water.

—John 7:38

We must keep our hearts pure to bring in the harvest in these last days!

Keeping transparency and openness to the Holy Spirit and others keeps our hearts in check and our motives pure. The flow of God is seen in everyone who purposely guards their hearts and asks for cleansing on a regular basis. *Help us to hear You, Lord, as the Holy Spirit prompts us to repent, as He convicts us of our sins.*

Pure love undefined is shapeless, formless, ready to expand and express itself. This kind of love is the kind that falls without effort, and sometimes without any warning. It is just undeniable love for whatever or whomever the heart decides to express itself. It's a selfless kind of love.

When the heart is pure, it sees no evil in a person, only the need of that person. Whether the need is salvation, healing, or deliverance, or simply a yearning to belong to that person, it reflects the heart in its purest state, reaching out to mankind. This is when we show forth God's heart, as we show benevolence toward one another.

A pure heart will always crave righteousness in any situation. The pureness of heart is love-driven, not motive-driven. Because pureness reflects the holiness of God, and the fact that God is love, the only satisfaction of one who has a pure heart is that he pleases God, not man. His only heart-set mission is to live in God's presence and finish the work that He has assigned him to do. Jesus demonstrated this kind of pureness and reverence toward the work His Father assigned Him to do.

THE BE ATTITUDES

Jesus saith unto them, My meat is to do the will of him that sent me, and to finish his work.

—John 4:34

Unto the pure all things are pure: but unto them that are defiled and unbelieving is nothing pure; but even their mind and conscience is defiled.

—Titus 1:15

Our minds are open doors to our hearts. Guarding our hearts requires close attention to our thoughts. If we harbor thoughts of unforgiveness, which are evil thoughts toward others, it defiles our conscience and causes us to become callous to the promptings of the Holy Spirit. When we deny the existence of our faults, it causes them to submerge into a deeper part of the heart, called our subconscious. It becomes easier and easier for us to remain in that state. Thanks be unto God who gives us the victory in Christ Jesus! We can overcome a faulty heart by acknowledging our sins and repentance.

Create in me a clean heart, O God; and renew a right spirit within me. . . . Restore unto me the joy of thy salvation; and uphold me with thy free spirit. Then will I teach transgressors thy ways; and sinners shall be converted unto thee.

—Psalm 51:10–13

PURE EYESIGHT

Repentance brings forth an anointing that not only restores, cleanses, frees, and strengthens, but that anointing delivers us, because it's the anointing that destroys the yoke (Isaiah 10:27); this anointing never leaves. By sharing our testimony to others, that same anointing will destroy the yoke of bondage and can convert sinners to the Kingdom of God. It's the deliverance of the heart that brings forth pureness of mind.

Hearest thou what these say? And Jesus saith unto them, Yea; have ye never read, Out of the mouth of babes and sucklings thou hast perfected praise?

—Matthew 21:16

What made the praises perfect? A little child's heart is pure, without sinful motives, without reservations. They see through the eyes of pure love. Their innocence is shown by their pure love. It emanates from their very being. Their faith is indescribably without fault. They have no other reason to praise God except for their pure love for Him. Children never hold grudges; they may fall out with each other, but soon after, you will find them skipping along, holding hands, and playing with one another as if nothing ever happened. This is the purest form of love to have one toward another.

Why is purity in the heart important? It allows us access into the presence of God. "Blessed are the pure in heart: for they shall see God" (Matthew 5:8). I am reminded of Jesus when He was on the cross. The moment our sins were laid upon Him, He felt the separation from His Father. Although He personally did not sin, our sins and iniquities were carried away by His shed blood and His death on the cross. He became the sacrificial Lamb who took away our sins. God is holy, and when He sees the iniquities in our hearts, it causes Him to withdraw from us until we are cleansed.

> *If I regard iniquity in my heart, the LORD will not hear me.*
>
> **—Psalm 66:18**

Even so, when we have iniquity in our hearts, we ourselves become reluctant to pray or to seek God. Because of what Jesus did for us on the cross, however, we are able to come boldly before the throne of God, where we can obtain mercy. However, as Adam and Eve did in the Garden after they had sinned, we also try to hide from God.

A pure heart allows entrance into the presence of God, although it is often taken for granted, perceived as weakness by predators and manipulators. However, the people with whom you share your pure heart cannot deny the encounter of love without measure, which comes from being in the presence of God. It causes them to experience the love of God through you. As the scent of a rose after the freshness of the dew has fallen, the fragrance of purity overpowers any evil. It reaches the heart and immediately produces roots, which grow and produce fruit in time. Often it brings forth repentance from others who have done evil deeds.

PURE EYESIGHT

A pure heart is as rare as a shining gem found in the midst of a cleft of rocks. It is like finding a diamond in the rough and realizing its worth once purified and polished. It has a uniqueness of its own. The cut of the diamond can be considered a priceless treasure or jewel. Just as a diamond is strong and worthy of significance, so is a pure heart cut out of adversity.

Realizing that your pure heart is your strength and not a weakness is imperative. We must understand that when we guard our hearts and allow virtue to flow through us, we are more like Christ than ever before. Acknowledging this will help keep our minds sober, and actively casting down vain imaginations, the wiles of the devil, will help us to accomplish the mandate on our lives, given to us by God.

I can do all things through Christ who strengthens me.
—Philippians 4:13 NKJV

When we love what God loves and how He loves, this maturity in Christ becomes a virtue. When we delight ourselves in Him to this capacity, He will give us the desires of our hearts. His desires become our desires. His desire is to fulfill His plans for our lives and to bring us to the expected end that He has designed for us before we were formed in our mothers' wombs.

Having this virtue of a pure heart allows God to move through our lives in a continuous flow. We become conduits

THE BE ATTITUDES

for the Holy Spirit to share the love of God, healing, and deliverance to others while revealing the magnanimity of His resources and power coming straight from heaven above. The Kingdom of heaven touches earth with undeniable signs, wonders, and miracles as a witness of God's glory and the magnitude of His reign as King over all!

I'm reminded of the story of Lazarus, the brother of Mary and Martha, found in John 11:1–45. Lazarus and his sisters were friends of Jesus. Lazarus fell ill, and they sent for Jesus. Lazarus died before He could get there. Although Lazarus had been dead for four long days, Jesus asked them to roll back the stone from the cave where they had buried him. Because of His pure heart, He knew His Father would hear and answer Him with the miracle of the resurrection of Lazarus from the dead.

> *Then they took away the stone from the place where the dead was laid. And Jesus lifted up his eyes, and said, Father, I thank thee that thou hast heard me. And I knew that thou hearest me always: but because of the people which stand by I said it, that they may believe that thou hast sent me. And when he thus had spoken, he cried with a loud voice, Lazarus, come forth. And he that was dead came forth, bound hand and foot with graveclothes: and his face was bound about with a napkin. Jesus saith unto them, Loose him, and let him go.*
>
> **—John 11:41–44**

That same power is available to us today!

The glory of God can be felt, demonstrated, and seen through one who carries a pure heart. Love flows from breast to breast and is like a magnet that draws others, especially those who are in need. Love from a pure heart is contagious. It gives others the desire to change and become more like Jesus. There is a peace and a glory that surrounds you so that others can visibly see and tangibly feel it. It is like having a truth finder. It searches out the good, the DNA of God that is in every person, and it connects with God's love, which He placed in the core of man, causing the darkness to flee while simultaneously releasing the heart from the stony places of sin. This love from a pure heart purifies and replaces a stony heart with a heart of flesh that can hear from God once again!

The wonders of His glory, and His majesty in our lives helps us to keep a pure heart, and to do so, we must fill our minds with God's Word. Meditating on the Word of God keeps us fresh, with revelation knowledge of the Most High. It keeps our minds in perfect peace, even during trials and tribulations. It serves as a constant reminder of God's love and a reminder of His promises when trouble arises.

The Word of God serves as a buffer in life's situations, thereby keeping the mind and heart pure.

> *Every word of God is pure: he is a shield unto them that put their trust in him.*
>
> **—Proverbs 30:5**

THE BE ATTITUDES

Having a worldly view of a pure heart or developing our own sense of purity can be harmful to our spiritual growth. We cannot excuse wrongful thinking or allow the suggestions from the enemy to rule our hearts and minds. Let the Word of God be a mirror that gives true reflection that can lead to cleansing of the mind, heart, and soul, producing a pure heart and a right relationship toward God and our fellow man.

> *There is a generation that are pure in their own eyes, and yet is not washed from their filthiness.*
>
> **—Proverbs 30:12**

> *Finally, brethren, whatsoever things are true, whatsoever things are honest, whatsoever things are just, whatsoever things are pure, whatsoever things are lovely, whatsoever things are of good report; if there be any virtue, and if there be any praise, think on these things.*
>
> **—Philippians 4:8**

7

Blessings of Peace

Blessed are the peacemakers:
for they shall be called the children of God.
—Matthew 5:9

Jehovah Shalom is the Hebrew name that translates to the English phrase "The Lord is peace." Jesus is also referred to as the Prince of Peace. Receiving Jesus as our Lord and Savior transcends us from the burden of sin to being born again into the Kingdom of God by the Spirit. Our spirit becomes renewed, and we are refreshed by the cleansing blood of Jesus, which was shed on the cross for our redemption.

When I think of God's children, I can't help but think about His only begotten Son, called Jesus. Oh, how I love Jesus! I am reminded of His steadfast love and humility as He walked this earth to fulfill God's plan to bring about our salvation. Sweet Jesus, the name that is above every name!

THE BE ATTITUDES

> *Neither is there salvation in any other: for there is none other name under heaven given among men, whereby we must be saved.*
>
> **—Acts 4:12**

One of the names given to Him is the Prince of Peace (Isaiah 9:6). This simply means that Jesus is the Master of peace. The gospel of Mark tells a story that portrays Him in action as this prince. After having left the seaside, where He had taught the people many parables, Jesus and His disciples climbed into a ship to cross over to the other side of the sea. The Word says:

> *And when they had sent away the multitude, they took him even as he was in the ship. And there were also with him other little ships. And there arose a great storm of wind, and the waves beat into the ship, so that it was now full. And he was in the hinder part of the ship, asleep on a pillow: and they awake him, and say unto him, Master, carest thou not that we perish? And he arose, and rebuked the wind, and said unto the sea, Peace, be still. And the wind ceased, and there was a great calm. And he said unto them, Why are ye so fearful? how is it that ye have no faith?*
>
> **—Mark 4:36–40**

Let us delve into this little excerpt of Scripture and find the application of this to our own lives. First, we see there was always someone there to see the actions that were to

BLESSINGS OF PEACE

take place on their journey. As it was then, so it is now in our lives. There is always the opportunity to show the power of God and what faith in Him can do. The winds of life, or opposition, that may arise and cause a chain reaction of difficulties and situations can sometimes produce fear, anxiety, or uncertainty about whether or not we will pull through. Although the disciples were fearful, however, they recognized their dependency was upon God and His Son, Jesus, to make it through the storm. Having a personal relationship with Jesus, they knew He had the power to save them. Sometimes in our lives, it seems as if God is asleep, oblivious to our circumstances. But God said in His Word that He would never leave us nor forsake us. He neither slumbers nor sleeps. There is a resting place in Him. When the waves come and the billows roll, in times like these we must not push the panic button, but instead call on the name of Jesus in prayer.

My help cometh from the LORD, which made heaven and earth. He will not suffer thy foot to be moved: he that keepeth thee will not slumber. Behold, he that keepeth Israel shall neither slumber nor sleep.
—Psalm 121:2–4

As Jesus did when He got up from His rest, our actions should be the same: to take authority over the root of the problem—in this case it was the wind. He rebuked the wind and spoke peace over the situation. Because Jesus gave unto us the power to rebuke the enemy that causes

THE BE ATTITUDES

the problems in our lives, in His name, we can rebuke the chaos in our lives, speak to peace, and command the chaos to be still. What fascinated me was that in this verse of Scripture, Jesus spoke to peace as if it had a personality of its own.

As I meditated on this passage of Scripture, I saw a revelation I had never seen before. Peace in this situation could be considered a derivative of Jesus Himself. When you look up the word *derivative*, as a noun it means "something that is based on another source." Wow! Of course, you know this took me on another adventure with the Holy Spirit. I went all the way back to John 1:1–3: "In the beginning was the Word, and the Word was with God, and the Word was God. The same was in the beginning with God. All things were made by him; and without him was not any thing made that was made." Genesis 1:9–10 says, "And God said, Let the waters under the heaven be gathered together unto one place, and let the dry land appear: and it was so. And God called the dry land Earth; and the gathering together of the waters called he Seas: and God saw that it was good." Because Jesus is the Prince of Peace, when He began speaking creation into existence, He said, "Let there be," and out of chaos, creation brought forth peace.

We have already established in chapter 1 that when He spoke this word, "Be," He was spreading a portion of Himself throughout creation. So, this word, *be*, became perpetual. He is the Prince of Peace and the Source of all creation. Peace in the midst of the sea is simply a portion of His personality. In our lives, because He is omnipotent, omniscient, and omnipresent, He is a very present help in the time of trouble. He is in the midst of our lives, problems, and difficulties. When we speak peace into our lives, and into our brother and sisters' lives, we are speaking what already exists in the spirit realm. We are calling those things that are not, on earth, as though they were. This causes a reaction from God, which brings heaven to earth. When we speak peace in the name of Jesus, we are exercising the same authority He did when he said, "Peace, be still."

Behold, I give unto you power to tread on serpents and scorpions, and over all the power of the enemy: and nothing shall by any means hurt you.

—Luke 10:19

The wind disrupted the natural flow and calmness of the sea. There is a natural presence of peace in the movement of nature, sitting on the porch watching the day break, seeing the sun rise or set, or being out on the lake watching the ripples of water while the glistening sun shimmers across the surface of the water, or listening to the sound of the birds chirping as the wind gently blows across your face. There is an astounding presence of peace in the heavens and surrounding atmosphere. However, because Satan is the prince of the power of the air here on earth (that authority was surrendered unto him by Adam when he fell into sin in the Garden), Satan can sometimes use the natural

THE BE ATTITUDES

elements here on earth to cause destruction. Jesus said in John 10:10, "The thief cometh not, but for to steal, and to kill, and to destroy: I am come that they might have life, and that they might have it more abundantly." When we exercise our God-given authority, it causes an abundance of peace and provision to come into our lives and the lives of others. We are demonstrating our sonship, as well as the culture of heaven, in Christ.

We are heirs and joint-heirs with Christ. We have the same power and authority to use here on earth in the name of Jesus. As Jesus did while He was here on earth, we must operate in a pureness of love to bring forth peace. All these attributes are intertwined together and must operate in perfect harmony, as separate components, but out of the same mind, spirit, and pure heart.

> *And the peace of God, which passeth all understanding, shall keep your hearts and minds through Christ Jesus.*
>
> **—Philippians 4:7**

This verse of scripture is a reminder of the innate abilities that lie within us as believers in Christ. The peacemaker is one who produces peace, or who creates peace within a given situation, especially during adverse conditions. When peace becomes a part of our personality, it resonates with heaven and brings forth joy unspeakable. It can be life-changing for others to see this kind of display of peace and joy. It is a fruit of the Spirit and is undeniable,

BLESSINGS OF PEACE

from the one who portrays it, and the ones who witness it in others. It's a state of being at rest in God. It is an inner God-given strength. The joy of the Lord provides us with strength to live peaceably among men.

> *But as many as received him, to them gave he power to become the sons of God, even to them that believe on his name.*
>
> **—John 1:12**

In a society where the culture of the day is violence, corruption, immorality, and every evil work, calling good evil and evil good, Jesus sends us as peacemakers to reconcile the world back to a standard of morality and good ethics.

In Christendom, we call it holiness. We are the equilibrium that brings balance in an unstable world. Jesus is the Mediator between God and man, so we, as diplomats, or ambassadors of the Kingdom of heaven, must also mediate through fasting and prayer, standing up for righteousness and speaking the truth. Spreading the good news of Jesus Christ gives hope to those who cannot see their way through. When hope is given, peace descends. Sharing the Gospel of Christ, the good news that there is a Way out, a Burden Bearer, and salvation for their lives, brings an inner peace and joy.

If you need peace today, know that God is only one prayer away. My grandmother said it like this: "Baby, He is a handsome Gentleman. He will not enter your situation unless you ask Him to come in."

> *Behold, I stand at the door, and knock: if any man hear my voice, and open the door, I will come in to him, and will sup with him, and he with me.*

—Revelation 3:20

If you prefer to go to Him, He said, "Come unto me, all ye that labour and are heavy laden, and I will give you rest" (Matthew 11:28); "ask, and it shall be given you; seek, and ye shall find; knock, and it shall be opened unto you: for every one that asketh receiveth; and he that seeketh findeth; and to him that knocketh it shall be opened" (Matthew 7:7–8).

In a world of unrest like we are living in today, people are looking for answers to their problems. As peacemakers, we are to seek out opportunities to provide the solution. Christ is the Answer to all our problems! As God's extended hands, when we reach out to others with benevolent acts of kindness, we will undoubtedly speak peace. This will cause doors to open for the Gospel of Jesus Christ to be preached. A snowball effect of blessings will begin to overflow. I am personally praying for the outpouring of God's Spirit and the manifestation of signs, wonders, and miracles in the earth like never seen before!

As God's peacemakers, we will be the first recipients of this grace. As His sons and daughters, we will become the conduits of this outpouring. We will be entrusted with

BLESSINGS OF PEACE

His glory of this magnitude to show forth His majesty here on the earth. As Jesus practiced all these attributes of His Father here on earth and revealed the Kingdom of God, so will we. I encourage you, as I am also doing, to learn of His ways, and to make it an everyday experience to walk according to the Spirit and the Kingdom of God. To participate in this last outpouring before His return, our lives must mirror Christ, reflecting the Father's love, compassion, humility, and His will for our lives. I am so excited to take this extended journey with Him. *Thank You, Lord, for choosing me in this last hour!*

> *And it shall come to pass afterward, that I will pour out my spirit upon all flesh; and your sons and your daughters shall prophesy, your old men shall dream dreams, your young men shall see visions: and also upon the servants and upon the handmaids in those days will I pour out my spirit. And I will shew wonders in the heavens and in the earth, blood, and fire, and pillars of smoke.*
>
> **—Joel 2:28–30**

> *But as it is written, Eye hath not seen, nor ear heard, neither have entered into the heart of man, the things which God hath prepared for them that love him. But God hath revealed them unto us by his Spirit: for the Spirit searcheth all things, yea, the deep things of God.*
>
> **—1 Corinthians 2:9–10**

Lord, I pray that You will open the eyes of our understanding so that we might see and perceive what it is that You by Your Holy Spirit are trying to reveal to us in this last dispensation of Your Spirit. Give unto us a heart of flesh that we might be able to discern and to absorb Your Word as You speak to us divine revelations. Help us to see You and the movement of the Holy Spirit by divine encounters revealing truth. You are truth, and only with spiritual eyes can we see, only if You open our ears can we hear what the Spirit is speaking to us in this last hour.

There are at least three areas of peace that we will visit. Visiting these areas is essential, because to become an effective peacemaker, we must first have peace in every area of our own lives. True peace and harmony begin within ourselves. These three areas are emotional peace, spiritual peace, and relational peace.

Let us begin with the deep things first. Because we tend to think of the natural before the spiritual, we will start with the emotions, which are the deep set or core of our very being. If we cannot contain our emotions, there will be an immediate disruption in our peace.

Five areas of emotions that will directly affect our attitudes toward life include anger, fear, sadness, disgust, and enjoyment. These we will call the "colors of our attitudes."

Red: Anger

While there are many more, we will focus on what I believe are the driving forces behind all the rest. Understanding our emotions is an important part of our spiritual and mental health. If we can conquer these areas, our role as a peacemaker will be a cinch. The first color is *red*, representing anger. We will take that red of anger and transform it with the red blood of Jesus. This transformation will result in the renewing of our mind.

Acknowledging that it is the Holy Spirit who works in us, both to will and to do of His good pleasure, is the first step to having eternal peace in our souls while here on earth. Yielding ourselves to the promptings of the Holy Spirit will keep us in perfect peace. As our spiritual Guide, Helper, and Comforter, it is His joy to bring back to our remembrance the Word of God, which keeps us and sustains us, keeping us from all unrighteousness. Anger clouds the mind when not in check, and it opens the door for sin. It can easily escalate into wrath. Whereas anger is a natural response to an event, lingering anger turns into the spirit called wrath, which can easily be provoked into behavioral things in the body that will result in sin. This is why they label certain actions of violence as "acts of passion." Meditating on the Word of God can help reduce our having a reaction to the actions of others.

THE BE ATTITUDES

Applying what I call the three RRRs will curb the desire to react and restrain us from doing evil. When you are provoked in a situation, before acting out, *relax*, take a deep breath, and listen to the Holy Spirit; *relate* to what will happen if you continue in that vein of thought; and *release* your will to God's will as the Holy Spirit reminds you of God's Word. You will find it refreshing to know that you did not allow the temptation of the enemy to overtake you, but by yielding your will to God's will, you decided to take the way of escape instead. You have just become more than a conqueror! You can apply this to any situation.

> *There hath no temptation taken you but such as is common to man: but God is faithful, who will not suffer you to be tempted above that ye are able; but will with the temptation also make a way to escape, that ye may be able to bear it.*
>
> **—1 Corinthians 10:13**

Write the following scripture down, put it in a beautiful frame and hang it throughout your house and in your car, to keep you motivated into good works:

> *Finally, brethren, whatsoever things are true, whatsoever things are honest, whatsoever things are just, whatsoever things are pure, whatsoever things are lovely, whatsoever things are of good report; if there be any virtue, and if there be any praise, think on these things. Those things, which ye have*

both learned, and received, and heard, and seen in me, do: and the God of peace shall be with you.

—Philippians 4:8–9

Father, let us not be conformed to the ways of this world, but help us to be transformed by the renewing of our minds, so that we might walk in the fruit of the Spirit of meekness, love, and gentleness, which produces peace. Help us to be more like You each day. Help us to look beyond the faults of others and see their need for healing and deliverance, in Jesus' name.

Black: Fear

There is no fear in love; but perfect love casteth out fear: because fear hath torment. He that feareth is not made perfect in love.

—1 John 4:18

God created us in His image. According to the Word, God is love. His whole essence is engulfed by His love. In this love, there is wholeness, wellness, peace, and harmony. Nothing missing Nothing lacking. In the Garden of Eden, Adam and Eve were lacking nothing. God had supplied every one of their needs. Their total trust was in Him. He covered them from all hurt, harm, and danger. You might say they lived a sheltered life in total bliss. They had everything imaginable, and they were totally dependent upon God and all the things He had provided for them. They knew no sin. Life was pure, peaceful, and full of tranquility. You could even call it *utopia*; I would call it "heaven on earth." It wasn't until the serpent, used by Satan, came, beguiled them, and caused them to lose their trust in God's love for them, that they became fearful. This was a time of darkness for them; they had lost their way. We will call it the color of black. The Bible says in Genesis 3:8 that after they had sinned, they hid from God. There are areas in our lives where this strongman called fear has crept in. If you cannot tell where this spirit is lurking in your life, pray and ask the Holy Spirit to reveal it to you. Often this spirit enters our lives when we are children. He then masks himself until we become adults. It is then we can see or feel that something is not quite right in our lives. We sometimes find ourselves fearful, not being able to trust God, His Word, or anyone else for that matter. When we are fearful, just like Adam and Eve, we tend to hide, because down on the inside we feel we are going to fail. The acronym for *FEAR* is *false evidence appearing real*. Fear will cause you to be stuck, too afraid to move forward. Stuck, wondering how you are going to make it tomorrow, when tomorrow is not promised. Fear disturbs your peace by causing worry to torment your mind.

Be anxious for nothing—the same God who took care of Adam and Eve after they had sinned, who literally stitched some clothes and dressed them, is the same Father who loves you so much. He will always keep His promise of provision for you.

BLESSINGS OF PEACE

Be careful for nothing; but in every thing by prayer and supplication with thanksgiving let your requests be made known unto God. And the peace of God, which passeth all understanding, shall keep your hearts and minds through Christ Jesus.

—Philippians 4:6–7

Beloved, if God so loved us, we ought also to love one another. No man hath seen God at any time. If we love one another, God dwelleth in us, and his love is perfected in us.

—1 John 4:11–12

Not only should we put our trust in God, but we should not be afraid to open to others. God will place divine connections in our lives, those whom He ordained to take us to the next level, but if we are too fearful to receive them, we will miss what God has intended. We are destiny helpers one to another. Let God's perfect love flow through you to bring peace to others in this world. To let love flow, you must become vulnerable, trusting God's lead. As you trust Him more and more, He will fill you with His love until it overflows, leaving no room for fear.

There is no fear in love; but perfect love casteth out fear: because fear hath torment. He that feareth is not made perfect in love.

—1 John 4:18

THE BE ATTITUDES

Father, we surrender our fears to You. No longer will we worry about tomorrow. We may not know what the future holds, but we know that You hold our future. From this day forward, we let go, and we let God. We pray for divine destiny helpers, divine connections to come into our lives, and that we may become helpers to others by Your love. Perfect Your love in us and through us, in Jesus' name!

Blue: Sadness and Disgust

> *Arise, shine; for thy light is come, and the glory of the LORD is risen upon thee. For, behold, the darkness shall cover the earth, and gross darkness the people: but the LORD shall arise upon thee, and his glory shall be seen upon thee.*

—Isaiah 60:1–2

These verses of Scripture describe both the darkness that can bring sadness into our lives and the contrast of light that always overpowers darkness. We can choose to be sad about all the trials and misfortunes that seemingly have overtaken our lives, or we can put our trust in God, who daily supply us with benefits. His Word tells us to arise, or to physically move in an upward direction. When feelings of sadness and depression come, it will literally lift our spirits when we leap up and start moving. The word *arise* can also mean "flow." When we press our way into life, it causes a cerebral effect, or a flow that gives the brain an uplift. We make an intelligent decision to choose to live

108

life, come what may. We begin to think on the bright side, so to speak, or we determine to cope with our new situations. The light that comes, or the glory we experience, is God's love, reaching out to comfort us. Although the sun is a natural light, here on earth, just to sit in the sun or the light causes the whole world and our life situations to become brighter. When the light hits our eyes, it connects with the light of God that's down in our souls. When we allow the Lord to move into our situations, it resonates with peace within us, so much so that others can see it and feel it.

The blue areas of our lives must be healed before we can bring peace to others. Our brokenness can also be seen and felt by others. Often, sadness comes from disappointments in life or our expectations of others that have been crushed by betrayal. Maybe it is because we have waited for so long for something to change in our lives. The enemy can trick us and cause us to be disgusted with ourselves, have feelings of failure, or even to give up on life itself. Maybe you've become disgusted by the offenses of others and closed yourself off from everything and everybody. There is light at the other end of the tunnel and hope for the dismayed that brings life.

> *Hope deferred maketh the heart sick: but when the desire cometh, it is a tree of life.*
> **—Proverbs 13:12**

THE BE ATTITUDES

*The thief cometh not, but for to steal, and
to kill, and to destroy: I am come that they
might have life, and that they might have it
more abundantly.*

—John 10:10

Let us put our hope in Jesus, who is the Author and
Finisher of our faith. It is He who has written the true story
of our lives. Trusting in Him to bring it to pass means
surrendering our emotions, our total life—to the Prince
of Peace. What better way to learn how to be an effective
peacemaker ourselves, but to follow His instructions found
in His Word. Allow the light of God to arise and shine upon
you, for His glory will be seen in your life!

*Wait on the LORD: be of good courage, and
he shall strengthen thine heart: wait, I say,
on the LORD.*

—Psalm 27:14

Lord Jesus, we surrender our emotions of sadness and
depression to You. You are Jehovah-Rapha, the God that
heals. We offer up our brokenness to You, praying that You
will heal our hearts, break down the walls that separate us
from destiny and purpose, and make us and mold us into
the vessels that You would have us to be. You are the Potter;
we are the clay. In Jesus' name, we pray!

Yellow: Enjoyment

Enjoyment means to enjoy the pleasures in life. When I think about the pleasures in life, I can't help but think about being in the presence of God. While this world may dictate pleasure as having riches, fame, fortune, and influence among men, there is nothing that can truly compare with being rich in God and having a continuous flow of His presence, by the Holy Spirit. All the worldly things and the lusts thereof may be pleasurable for a moment, but the joy of the Lord is an everlasting joy. Many have made it to the top of life's mountain, only to find themselves empty, miserable, and if the truth be told, lonely.

There is a hiding place in God that is higher than any place the world can ever take you. It is called "in His Presence." It is indescribable, and to many who have never experienced Him before, it is unconceivable, but to those who *have* tapped into Him, it is truly tangible and undeniable. The gentleness of His touch and warm embrace fills you up with a love that embraces your very soul and leaves no room for the word *empty*. In fact, it's the very opposite—and much, much more.

There is an overflow that takes you into a world filled with peace, love, ecstasy, and enchantment. It's where you know that you are in this world, but not of this world. It's a place in Him that causes you to want more, never to leave, and to seek after daily. Once you have been in His Presence,

THE BE ATTITUDES

you realize there is no true enjoyment in life without Him. The greatest love you have ever known on earth, which brought nothing but joy to your life, cannot compare with this overwhelming love that causes your heart to become immersed with such a purity that it transforms yours into an everlasting joy and state of peace that it surpasses all understanding.

Whereas happiness is an emotion of enjoyment, it is contingent upon the circumstances that brought it about. When those circumstances are interrupted, so is happiness. The joy the Lord gives down in your soul from being in His presence—it is an everlasting joy that will bring enjoyment even during the trials, tribulations, and the storms of life. The joy of the Lord is our strength and will cause us to rise, especially in adversity, with victory.

Being in this place emotionally gives us an eternal enjoyment in life, and a broad perspective in terms of what true joy is. If I had to sum it all up in a nutshell, I would say that in this world we will always have some type of tribulation. But having the Lord in our lives will, indeed, help us in life situations. Receiving him as Lord and Savior comes with many benefits, but getting to know Him and being in His Presence daily will bring a contentment in your emotions and your soul that will fill you with unspeakable joy. To be anchored, steadfast, and unmovable, we must seek Him with our whole heart and be thankful daily. Staying in His Word builds an intimate relationship.

BLESSINGS OF PEACE

Having this type of enjoyment in life also causes the glory of God to rest upon us. People will see this peace, joy, and contentment and gravitate toward us, hoping to figure out what is that connection causing us to be so peaceful and full of joy and contentment. This will open the door for the gospel of Jesus Christ, the Prince of Peace. You will become the peacemaker in the room to many people. You will find that people will ask for your counsel in many situations, and because you dwell in His presence, you will be able to speak peace, healing, and deliverance into their lives.

When we meditate on His Word every day, it builds our relationship with Him so that you become inseparable. You will literally eat, sleep, walk, and breathe His total Presence. You will become engulfed and totally immersed in His glory. You become one with Him, full of His glory and love. There is an awareness of His Presence as He surrounds you, whispering truths, giving divine revelations as He shares His heart and mind. These truly are pleasures, and an enjoyment that only He can give. This color we will call yellow, for truly He is the sunshine (the Son who shines) that brightens our lives.

> *Father, we thank You for the ability to come into Your presence, for You said in Your Word, "Let us therefore come boldly unto the throne of grace, that we may obtain mercy, and find grace to help in time of need" (Hebrews 4:16). And, "Thou wilt shew me*

THE BE ATTITUDES

the path of life: in thy presence is fullness of joy; at thy right hand there are pleasures for evermore" (Psalm 16:11). We thank You for the enjoyment in life that You give to us so that we may find contentment, have peace, and share love with others. Teach us how to forever remain under the shadow of Your wings, in Jesus' name.

He that dwelleth in the secret place of the most High shall abide under the shadow of the Almighty. He shall cover thee with his feathers, and under his wings shalt thou trust: his truth shall be thy shield and buckler.

—Psalm 91:1 4

Spiritual Peace

Spiritual peace cannot be attained by mere mortal standards alone. To obtain this peace, we must put on immortality. I can hear you asking, How can I do that? A similar question was asked in the Bible by Nicodemus. Jesus answered him by saying:

Verily, verily, I say unto thee, Except a man be born again, he cannot see the kingdom of God. Nicodemus saith unto him, How can a man be born when he is old? can he enter the second time into his mother's womb, and be born? Jesus answered, Verily verily, I say unto thee, Except a man be born of water and of the Spirit, he cannot enter into the

BLESSINGS OF PEACE

kingdom of God. That which is born of the flesh is flesh, and that which is born of the Spirit is spirit.

—John 3:3–6

Being born of water and of Spirit is representation of the cleansing power of His Word. Christ gave Himself for us that He might sanctify and cleanse us with the washing of water by His Word. He is the Word, and by receiving the message of the good news and salvation, we have passed from death to life. To receive this washing as God has designed for our salvation and reconciliation, it is as simple as one . . . two . . . three.

Acknowledging that Jesus died on the cross for our sins, it is the repentance of our sins, and receiving Jesus into our hearts, making Him our Lord and Savior, that cleanses us from all unrighteousness. We are then changed by the Holy Spirit, undergoing a spiritual birth, newness of life, being birthed into the Kingdom of God. We have now passed from the stain of sin, which is death, into eternal life in Christ Jesus, where we have peace.

Therefore if any man be in Christ, he is a new creature: old things are passed away; behold, all things are become new.

—2 Corinthians 5:17

Receiving Christ is the first step in obtaining peace. We have now been reconciled back to the Father, in right standing, because of the shed blood of Jesus, and into

THE BE ATTITUDES

the safety of His loving arms. Although we are yet in our mortal body, our spirit has taken on immortality. We now have access into heaven to live throughout eternity with Jesus. Thank God for His amazing grace! Spiritual peace is taking God at His Word—if He said it, that settles it. He is not a man that He should lie. In Christ, the promise of God is yes, and amen. Finding that resting place in Him means trusting that whatever comes into our lives, good or bad, God is faithful to us, His children. This signifies our affirmation of, and trust in, this given faithfulness from Him. Finally, knowing that we have eternal peace and a place in His Kingdom secures a peace of mind as to our destination when we transition from this present life here on earth into our final resting place with Him.

> *For all the promises of God in him are yea, and in him Amen, unto the glory of God by us.*
> **—2 Corinthians 1:20**

> *Let not your heart be troubled: ye believe in God, believe also in me. In my Father's house are many mansions: if it were not so, I would have told you. I go to prepare a place for you. And if I go and prepare a place for you, I will come again, and receive you unto myself; that where I am, there ye may be also.*
> **—John 14:1–3**

Father, we thank You for giving us Your Son, Jesus Christ, to die for our sins. Thank You for the ability to be

BLESSINGS OF PEACE

freed from sin and the turmoil of this world. Because of Jesus, we now have a resting place in You, where we can have peace during the storms in life. Thank You for the double peace in our lives—eternal peace and peace here on earth. Help us to share this loving grace with others, in Jesus' name, amen.

Relational Peace

Master, which is the great commandment in the law? Jesus said unto him, Thou shalt love the Lord thy God with all thy heart, and with all thy soul, and with all thy mind. This is the first and great commandment. And the second is like unto it, Thou shalt love thy neighbor as thyself. On these two commandments hang all the law and the prophets.

—Matthew 23:36–40

Therefore all things whatsoever ye would that men should do to you, do ye even so to them: for this is the law and the prophets.

—Matthew 7:12

These two sets of Scriptures go hand in hand and are the foundational Scriptures for relationship.

"Love thy neighbor as thyself" is the Golden Rule. Gold is the most precious mineral we have on earth and apparently also in heaven. According to the Scriptures, the streets in heaven are paved in gold. Our relationships here

THE BE ATTITUDES

on earth are just as precious to God. God loved us so much He decided to use His own hands to shape us and mold us from the dust of the ground, into His own image. He wanted us to be so much like Him that He personally breathed into Adam's nostrils the breath of life, and he *be*came a living soul. It was the deposit of His own DNA that brought life into man and caused him to *be*, or to exist. So, the question is, how can we separate the God in us from the man that was created? Seeing that it is ultimately impossible to do so, we must always recollect the fact that whatever we do to others, or however we treat our brothers and sisters called our neighbors, we have done it unto God. This was the awakening revelation of the Scriptures above that the Holy Spirit revealed to me.

It gets even deeper. The first thing He said about relationships with others was to be just as loving to others as we are to ourselves. It is God's desire that we have relational peace with ourselves, and that we love on ourselves, realizing that we are made in His image.

> *I will praise thee; for I am fearfully and wonderfully made: marvelous are thy works; and that my soul knoweth right well.*
> **—Psalms 139:14**

In Hebrew, this set of Scriptures refers to God's great reverence, heartfelt interest, and the respect He has for us. Because we are His children and not robots off an assembly line, He took the utmost care in giving each of us our own personalized set of DNA of Himself. Because of the greatness of His power and the vastness of Himself, He gave each of us a unique version of Himself.

> *For you created my inmost being; you knit me together in my mothers' womb. My frame was not hidden from you when I was made in the secret place, when I was woven together in the depths of the earth. Your eyes saw my unformed body; all the days ordained for me were written in your book before one of them came to be.*
>
> **—Psalm 139:13, 15–16** NIV

By His own choice, He created you beautiful in every way, fit for the purpose that only you and your awesome set of abilities that He entrusted in you can accomplish. To condemn ourselves for any reason is totally against the will of God. Who we were made to be, how we look, where we were born, and yes, even the family into which we were born, was all a part of His master plan. Even when we feel we have fallen short, we must still love who we are, and trust the plan that God has designed for our uniqueness. To love God is to love ourselves, and to love ourselves just as God created us is to love God and to trust His plan for our lives.

> *"For I know the plans I have for you," declares the* LORD, *"plans to give you hope and a future."*
>
> **—Jeremiah 29:11** NIV

THE BE ATTITUDES

For I know the thoughts that I think towards you, saith the LORD, thoughts of peace, and not of evil, to give you an expected end.

—Jeremiah 29:11 KJV

Father, help us so that when we look at ourselves, we will see You and know that You love us so much that You created us to be who we are, a unique version of You. Help us to forgive and love ourselves as You forgave us for our sins, in Jesus' name.

Having peace within yourself is respecting and loving the God in you. Relational peace can only be attained by having a personal relationship with God to the extent of having respect for His divine creation—beginning with yourself. Knowing that He designed us to portray an aspect of His wisdom, character, and creativity on the earth alone demands the utmost reverence and respect. Laying all negativity and condemning thoughts from the enemy aside, looking in the mirror and acknowledging the craftiness of His handiwork, the wisdom and wonders of His glory that dwells inside of us, should amaze us to the point of giving honor and glory to His wonderful name! He is the Creator and Sustainer of the universe.

As He reveals Himself in me and through me each and every day, I am in awe, and I recognize the majesty that dwells inside of me. I am at peace, knowing His love for me and experiencing His divine will for my life as I surrender myself totally to the plan that He has designed for me from

BLESSINGS OF PEACE

the foundation of the world. Developing a close relationship with Him and yielding myself to the Holy Spirit has caused me not only to love and respect the God in me and myself, but also to love those around me, knowing He loves them just as much as He loves me. Because of the part of Him that is within them, I cannot help but love God's people. We are all His children, created in His image for a divine purpose here on this earth. Realizing that my neighbors are my sisters and brothers in Christ Jesus has caused my heart to swell with empathy and love.

Having this alone is not enough; we should get involved in others' lives to help strengthen them where needed. To reach out with the love of God and tell them of His goodness and mercy toward them. To use the giftings and authority in the name of Jesus that He has given to us to break the bonds of the enemy off their lives. To fight for them through prayer and as the Holy Spirit leads. To speak peace into their lives. To share the blessings that God has given to us, however great or small. To be a conduit of God's blessings and love to others. To help one could mean helping thousands, for we know not the gifts and calling upon their lives. This is relational peace—to love one another as Christ has loved us.

Greater love hath no man than this, that a man lay down his life for his friends.
—John 15:13

THE BE ATTITUDES

And we have known and believed the love that God hath to us, God is love; and he that dwelleth in love dwelleth in God, and God in him. If a man say, I love God, and hateth his brother, he is a liar: for he that loveth not his brother whom he hath seen, how can he love God whom he hath not seen?

—1 John 4:16, 20

Hereby perceive we the love of God, because he laid down his life for us: and we ought to lay down our lives for the brethren. But whoso hath this world good, and seeth his brother have need, and shutteth up his bowels of compassion from him, how dwelleth the love of God in him? My little children, let us not love in word, neither in tongue; but in deed.

—1 John 3:16–18

Lord, help us to love our neighbors, considering the love that You have shown us. The love that looked beyond our faults and saw our needs. Thank You for Your patience and faithfulness, and for not giving up on us. Help us to see others through the eyes of the Spirit, and to love others as You have loved us. Give us the wisdom to win others to Christ so that they may share in the peace and love You have given unto us. Give unto us a heart of charity and compassion. It is for this reason that You came. In Jesus' name. Amen.

For God so loved the world, that he gave his only begotten Son, that whosoever believeth in him should not perish, but have everlasting life.

—John 3:16

By this shall all men know that ye are my disciples, if ye have love one to another.

—John 13:35

Relational peace comes with knowing the love of God that surpasses all understanding, the kind of love that never dissipate or changes. Hebrews 13:8 tells us that "Jesus Christ [is] the same yesterday, and to day, and for ever." His love is unconditional, meaning we can never merit or earn God's love; it was there from the beginning, and it will never be removed. This is a love that carries on throughout eternity and beyond our wildest dreams. God is a good Father who cares enough about us that Jesus humbled Himself from the state of being the Creator and Sustainer of the universe, to involving Himself in the affairs of man, giving purpose to our lives. This love helps guide us into our destiny to fulfill that purpose. The love of the Father extends far greater than any human capacity. Even when we are unfaithful, He is yet faithful, and He loves us enough to draw us back into His plan for our lives by His grace and mercy. If God can love us unconditionally in spite of our proclivities, how much more should we love one another?

We as parents should identify with the love that our

THE BE ATTITUDES

heavenly Father gives unto us and duplicate it in the lives of our children, recognizing them as being a blessing sent from heaven above. Having a child is having an heir, or an extension of oneself, as a continuation of glory in the earth, representing our Father in heaven through our lineage. Love should be the motivation to nurture them, shield and protect them, provide for them, and train them up in the admonition of the Lord. As Jesus came to the earth to show us the way, parents should also set an example in the Lord for their children. Being responsible and reflecting this kind of love automatically invokes a home filled with a sense of security, love, and peace. There is a respect that comes with this type of caring, and great family relationships are born out of this kind of environment.

Loving others outside of the family can be considered as God's extended family to us. If you really think about it, in the beginning God made Adam and Eve and blessed them. He told them to be fruitful and multiply. Generations later, here we are, one big happy family, as this was what God intended. Sin came in and caused separation, first man from God, then the breakdown of the family. Having been reconciled back to God through Christ, who gave Himself for our sins, we are no longer strangers, but we are joint heirs with Christ.

> *And he is the propitiation for our sins: and not for ours only, but also for the sins of the whole world.*
>
> **—1 John 2:2**

BLESSINGS OF PEACE

For ye have not received the spirit of bondage again to fear; but ye have received the Spirit of adoption, whereby we cry, Abba, Father. The Spirit itself beareth witness with our spirit, that we are the children of God: and if children, then heirs; heirs of God, and joint heirs with Christ; if so be that we suffer with him, that we may be also glorified together.

—Romans 8:15–17

Having relational love, which brings about relational peace, is God's heart for all of creation. Standing up for the rights of others, having respect for their humanity and the God who lives inside of them, will bring peace one to another. Relational peace is also extended toward God's creation. Having abused the use of everything He created for the provision, peace, and tranquility of man has caused chaos and undue upheaval of the planet's resources, as well as having caused climate change and unrest to the many threatened extinctions of His creatures and creation. Restoring the respect and love toward the people, the natural resources, and the world itself will provoke relational peace with man and all of creation.

Heavenly Father, help us to be the kind of peacemakers who will love enough to restore the broken places in our lives and others. Help us to seek opportunities to help bring peace in others' lives. Open our eyes of understanding as how to replenish and bring peace back to the resources that You have provided for our survival here on this earth, in Jesus' name.

THE BE ATTITUDES

Above all, having love, compassion, and understanding toward our family can give us the greatest rewards toward relational peace. To make amends, whatever the reason for the fallout with family, will create an everlasting bond thicker than ceramic glue. Because of the sin of Adam, we became estranged from the Father, but because of the shed blood of Christ, we are reconciled back into His grace, and mercy has bonded us forever, sealing us with His Holy Spirit throughout eternity!

> *For I am persuaded, that neither death, nor life, nor angels, nor principalities, nor powers, nor things present, nor things to come, nor height, nor depth, nor any other creature, shall be able to separate us from the love of God, which is in Christ Jesus our Lord.*
>
> **—Romans 8:38–39**

When we have conquered these areas of our lives, overcoming by submission to the Holy Spirit as He leads and guides us, surrendering our will to the will and plan of God for our lives, we will have mastered relational peace in all humbleness of heart, and we will have become God's designated peacemakers as the children of God. *Thank You, Lord, for having chosen us.*

8

Righteous Blessings, Destiny Helpers

*Blessed are they which are persecuted for
righteousness' sake: for theirs is the kingdom of
heaven. Blessed are ye, when men shall revile you,
and persecute you, and shall say all manner of evil
against you falsely, for my sake. Rejoice, and be
exceeding glad: for great is your reward in heaven:
for so persecuted they the prophets
which were before you.*
—Matthew 5:10–12

Rejoice, and again I say, rejoice! There is a joy attached
to being persecuted for standing up for the principles of
God in Christ Jesus. When the world count us out for
showing God's sovereignty, His holiness, and His steadfast
love by living according to His Word as best we know how,
it is time to rejoice and be exceedingly glad, for this is a
test of your induction into the Kingdom of heaven. The
world loves its own, but we as Christians are in this world,

THE BE ATTITUDES

but not of this world. Persecution for righteousness only stamps heaven's approval upon our lives.

> *The apostles left the Sanhedrin, rejoicing because they had been counted worthy of suffering disgrace for the Name.*
>
> **—Acts 5:41** NIV

Sometimes persecution can be cruel, vicious, and even diabolical as we walk in the pattern of our Lord and Savior, Jesus Christ. The Bible tells us to "be sober, be vigilant; because your adversary the devil, as a roaring lion, walketh about, seeking whom he may devour" (1 Peter 5:8). Even in the midst of our enemies, we are taught to love unconditionally, recognizing that they are caught in the snare of the enemy and are being used as puppets. We as the children of God must show forth the mercy of God and pray for them. We who are called by His name must contend for their deliverance through prayer, showing love. As hard as it may sound, and most of the time is, loving them will draw them into heaven's gates much more quickly than retaliation.

> *The LORD hath appeared of old unto me, saying, Yea, I have loved thee with an everlasting love: therefore with lovingkindness have I drawn thee.*
>
> **—Jeremiah 31:3**

> *But I say unto you, Love your enemies, bless*
> *them that curse you, do good to them that hate*
> *you, and pray for them which despitefully use*
> *you, and persecute you.*

—Matthew 5:43–44

How can we do these things? With our natural abilities we cannot, but when we submit our abilities to God's ability, he puts His *super* on our *natural* and gives us a *supernatural* love that comes straight from the Holy Spirit into our hearts—and we become like Him. Hope for their deliverance arises, and we are able to look beyond their faults and see their needs.

> *And hope maketh not ashamed; because the*
> *love of God is shed abroad in our hearts by*
> *the Holy Ghost which is given unto us.*

—Romans 5:5

Satan's desire is to cause us to stumble and utterly fall into sin and degradation. He is the accuser of the brethren, meaning he will use whomever he find as an open vessel to provoke us to act out in a sinful way, to bring accusation against us before God. When we retaliate against our attackers, we reduce ourselves to their level, and therefore we are identifying with Satan's sin nature instead of the righteousness of God. We are inadvertently portraying the character of Satan instead of the character of Christ. This can easily send mixed messages to the unbeliever.

THE BE ATTITUDES

We are ambassadors of Christ, and our lives must mirror the life of Christ, not knowing whose life will be changed through our obedience. *Lord, help us to take up our cross daily and follow after You, in Jesus' name.*

Persecution can come in many forms; therefore, a daily heart check, and a cleansing repentance prayer for sins of both omission and commission, is pertinent to remain in a mindset that reflects purity as a follower of Christ. If we allow persecution to affect us personally, our spirituality will become tainted with the stain of sin. Because of the lies, ostracism, hostility, ill treatment, intimidation, or even harassment that comes along with persecution, we may find ourselves loaded down with the spirit of offense, rejection, unforgiveness, and finally bitterness, which can easily lead to hatred. Let's take a closer look at these traps set by the enemy of our souls.

When we become entangled with a yoke of bondage, it usually starts with one open entry, or doorway, in our lives. One of the easiest ways the enemy gains entrance into our lives is through our emotions. The spirit of offense is a grand master of deception, lies, and propaganda, whose entire and only purpose is to deliberately damage, or bring injury to, the cause of Christ. Because we are carriers of God's glory, this spirit seeks out opportunities to cause an offense to occur. When entrapped by this diabolical spirit, it becomes what is called a strongman in our lives, or the entry point for strongholds or other spirits to enter. Because

Satan has no originality, he is always a copycat. He can only try to duplicate what's already been established in heaven.

> *There are three that bear record in heaven,*
> *the Father, the Word, and the Holy Ghost:*
> *and these three are one.*
>
> **—1 John 5:7**

God is one in essence, but three in Person. We are a triune being, made up of a spirit, the part of us that connects with God; a soul, which includes the mind or intellect, the emotions, and the will, the decision-making parts; and the body, the portion that houses everything while we are here on earth. Mimicking the creation of God, oftentimes the enemy moves in threes, meaning if there is one demonic presence, nine times out of ten there are at least two others, with the three hanging all together. So, the strong man enters our lives using offense as a weapon against our emotions, which lie in our soulish ram. After it has gained entrance, it brings at least two or three other spirits with it, frequently the spirits of rejection and unforgiveness. Under the influence of these spirits, we find ourselves operating according to the nature of Satan, our archenemy, instead of walking in righteousness and the nature of God. Just as the anointing on our lives from the Holy Spirit flows to others, so does the poison of unforgiveness, rejection, and offense. We began to see life through the wrong lenses, which strips away the joy of our salvation, and the root seed of bitterness begins to grow. Not only does it grow, but it can be seen and heard throughout our conversations, and our reactions toward others. Because we usually are not able to detect these spirits in our own lives, we become pessimistic instead of optimistic concerning things in our lives. We no longer are able to encounter a true relationship with God.

Those who practice witchcraft oftentimes use the weapon or tactic of offense to entrap our destiny and purpose. It is like being trapped in a spiderweb, spun from lies and slander—we are making motions or movement, but going nowhere. We become stagnated in our purpose, focusing on the offenses instead of the call of God on our lives. Because they usually follow up this offense with alienation, rejection sets in and takes up its course in our lives, causing us to become null to the voice of the Holy Spirit as He tries to bring about our deliverance. Recognizing the workings of these spirits and reaching out to others for prayer to be delivered is crucial. A stronghold is simply that—an area of your life that's being held hostage by demonic forces and in need of deliverance. To continue without deliverance takes us deeper into the clutch of the enemy. At this point, unforgiveness can easily set in our hearts, which can not only affect our spiritual life, but also has adverse effects on our mental, emotional, and physical self. Our entire focus becomes engulfed with the lies and ill treatment of the offenders. We tend to tell everyone we meet about the abusive treatment we are having to endure. This leads to what is called a root seed of bitterness, whose

RIGHTEOUS BLESSINGS, DESTINY HELPERS

root is extended deeper into our hearts as we hold on to and nurture the offense. That seed is distributed to others every time we bring up the subject. We find ourselves spreading the kingdom of darkness instead of the Kingdom of light. It does not matter if you have a title or position, the more affluent you are will only affect and undoubtedly infect more people if not put in check. I am writing these things to expose the enemy's encampment in your life, and I am praying for your deliverance now, in Jesus' name.

But there is light at the end of the tunnel! Your destiny is not lost. If you recognize yourself in this scenario, all you have to do is acknowledge your sin; repent, or turn away from it; and call on the name of Jesus. Renounce having been involved with the workings of these spirits, take your God-given authority over them, and command them to leave your presence, in Jesus' name. Your next step is to earnestly pray for those who have wronged you, giving the thoughts of revenge over to the Lord and asking Him to fill you with His love for them.

> *Dearly beloved, avenge not yourselves, but rather give place unto wrath: for it is written, Vengeance is mine; I will repay, saith the Lord. Therefore if thine enemy hunger, feed him; if he thirst, give him drink: for in so doing thou shalt heap coals of fire on his head.*
> **—Romans 12:19–20**

THE BE ATTITUDES

Persecution in any form is a hard pill to swallow. When men start to revile you, or criticize you repeatedly in an abusive or insulting, angry way, it can become very demeaning. It is a cowardly move of the enemy to try to affect your psyche and strip away your confidence in yourself and the calling of God on your life. It is usually spun out of envy, jealousy, and the desire of others to control your life. Although it can seem harsh, God allows it and even uses it to thrust us into our destiny. It is His way of pruning us for the blessings that lie ahead. Those who came against us, in a roundabout way, become our destiny helpers.

> *And we know that all things work together for good to them that love God, to them who are the called according to his purpose.*
>
> **—Romans 8:28**

Father, we trust You, and we thank You for all things in our lives.

> *Rejoice, and be exceeding glad: for great is your reward in heaven for so persecuted they the prophets which were before you.*
>
> **—Matthew 5:12**

This promise of blessing supersedes anything here on earth. The enemy is a thief, but because God avenges us, he must pay back with interest what he has stolen during these times of persecution.

But if he be found, he shall restore sevenfold;
he shall give all the substance of his house.

—Proverbs 6:31

If it caused you to be stagnated for years, it may seem like you have lost it all, and that everything has dried up, but God has a recalculated, recalibrated, renewing, refreshing, restoring, repositioning rebirth designed just for you!

Be glad then, ye children of Zion, and rejoice in the LORD your God: for he hath given you the former rain moderately, and he will cause to come down for you the rain, the former rain, and the latter rain in the first month. And I will restore to you the years that the locust hath eaten, the cankerworm, and the caterpillar, and the palmerworm, my great army which I sent among you.

—Joel 2:23, 25

This blessing comes in exponential proportions, meaning it is multiplied excessively. It will become an outpouring that will overflow into eternity. This kind of blessing touches our lives, and everyone who comes into contact with us experiences great deliverances and manifestations as well!

In the life of a believer, there will be persecution. There is no way around it. Although it may seem like you are the target, it is the plan of God and the purpose for your life that the enemy is after. God's design incorporates all of

THE BE ATTITUDES

mankind like a big jigsaw puzzle. Every piece is needed for the overall picture to be complete. This is why the enemy does everything he can to block, stop, or totally annihilate the plan of God in our lives. The difference is that God is the Creator, so He can redesign the layout any way He chooses to accomplish the end result that He has planned. It is a win–win for you, me, and all those who put their trust in Jesus.

In these times of opposition, guard your hearts. Filter your thoughts, emotions, and desires through the Word of God. If it does not line up with the Word of God, you are acting and moving in the wrong spirit.

> *A good man out of the good treasure of his heart bringeth forth that which is good; and an evil man out of the evil treasure of his heart bringeth forth that which is evil: for of the abundance of the heart his mouth speaketh.*
>
> **—Luke 6:45**

We must be like Paul in these situations. He wrote:

> *Brethren, I count not myself to have apprehended: but this one thing I do, forgetting those things which are behind, and reaching forth unto those things which are before, I press toward the mark for the prize of the high calling of God in Christ Jesus.*
>
> **—Philippians 3:13–14**

RIGHTEOUS BLESSINGS, DESTINY HELPERS

Father, we thank You for revealing the areas of our lives where we need deliverance. Heal every wound the enemy afflicted in Jesus' name. Rekindle the joy of our salvation. Renew our minds and create in us a clean heart as You renew the right spirit within us, so that we can be an example for Your Kingdom and teach others in Your way. Send a refreshing from the Holy Spirit, in Jesus' name.

9

Savory Seasonings

*Ye are the salt of the earth: but if the salt have
lost his savour, wherewith shall it be salted? It is
thenceforth good for nothing, but to be cast out, and
to be trodden under foot of men.*

—Matthew 5:13

The comparison of salt to salvation in Christ is almost inconceivable. In this metaphor, Jesus refers to the Church, or the followers of Christ, as the salt of the earth. Salt in its natural form is a crystalline mineral that is composed primarily of sodium chloride ($NaCl$), a chemical compound, and is referred to as rock salt, or halite. Whereas there are many forms of salt, which ranges from different countries in the world, they all have one basic common denominator: They all can be used as a preservative. As a preservative, when salt is rubbed onto meat, its life expectancy is increased, and the death or the decay of the meat is prolonged. Many of our forefathers used this method of preserving meat that was hunted from the wildlife. In addition to salting, they placed the meat in what they called smokehouses. The smoking caused the salt to be embedded deep into the flesh of the animal. The combination of salt and the smoke extended the life of the meat until it could be cooked for the nourishment of the family.

Salt can also be beneficiary to our health in many ways. Some of the benefits of salt used for our health include the following: Sodium, another name for salt, is naturally contained in the body and is held inside and outside of the cells. Because the body is made up of at least 50 to 75 percent water, our good health depends on the balance of these salty waters. God in His infamous wisdom gave us a sodium-potassium pump system to keep this balance intact. It is His way of knowing and providing for what is needed for His creation. The human body is also made up of bones, nerves, muscles, and other components, and all these depend on salt as essential for their proper function. Salt can also be used as a means of communication in the body, for it helps nerve impulses, which are needed to signal the muscle called our brain, which then tells the body the action that needs to take place. It can cause the muscles to relax when needed. Oh, the wisdom of God! He is awesome in all His ways. The sodium in the human body maintains a proper balance of water and minerals, all essential to healthy living. Too much salt can throw things out of balance, causing a malfunction, and the same is true for too little salt. All must stay in balance according to the

SAVORY SEASONINGS

knowledge and wisdom of God upon the creation of the human body.

As we focus on the natural flow of salt in the earth, we should also be reminded of the heavenly flow or the spiritual flow that takes place in the unseen realms. The body of Christ is a body that is formed spiritually by the new birth in Christ, and it, too, has a flow that causes the Kingdom of heaven to properly be maintained or function in the earth. In John 3 (please read at your leisure), Jesus answers a question that was given to Him by a man called Nicodemus. This man made a valid statement as to his earthly beliefs, having seen and experienced what I call "divine encounters," as the Lord healed the sick and cast out devils. Because he was a Pharisee, which was a religious sect of that time, he came to Jesus by night to hear His words and to witness the miracles He was performing. In awe of what he saw, Nicodemus came to Jesus and said, "Rabbi, we know that thou art a teacher come from God: for no man can do these miracles that thou doest, except God be with him. Jesus answered and said unto him, Verily, verily, I say unto thee, Except a man be born again, he cannot see the kingdom of God" (John 3:2–3). Jesus was alluding to a culmination of spiritual elements, if you will, that is essentially needed to make up the body of Christ. Without these, there would be a malfunction in the proper participation and involvement of the body of Christ. Nicodemus was yet seeing Jesus as a teacher sent from God instead of as the promised Messiah. Jesus was appealing to

THE BE ATTITUDES

his intellect, and He began by introducing him to the proper balance of salt in the earth.

Nicodemus saith unto him, How can a man be born when he is old? Can he enter the second time into his mother's womb, and be born? Jesus answered, Verily, verily, I say unto thee, Except a man be born of water and of the Spirit, he cannot enter into the kingdom of God. That which is born of flesh is flesh; and that which is born of Spirit is spirit.

—

Here we see the comparison of the need for water and salt in the natural body working together, along with other minerals, for their proper function, to the water and salt along with other attributes in the spiritual body of Christ, to preserve its order of function.

The revelation of this given from the Holy Spirit is that in the natural, the mineral of salt was given as an additive, along with water in the body, to replicate a functioning system of the spirit realm, found in the Kingdom of heaven.

And God said, Let us make man in our image, after our likeness: and let them have dominion over the fish of the sea, and over the fowl of the air, and over the cattle, and over all of the earth, and over every creeping thing that creepeth over the earth. So God created man in his own image, in the image of God created

SAVORY SEASONINGS

he him; male and female created he them.
—Genesis 1: 26–27

God made a replica of Himself on earth in bodily form, as male, and later female, as you can read in Genesis 2:21–24. Let us continue in Genesis 1:7:

And the LORD God formed man of the dust of the ground, and breathed into his nostrils the breath of life; and man [Be-came] a living soul.

In other words, with a breath from His nostrils and the spoken word, "Be," the Lord gave man the creative functioning power of heaven, in an earthly form. We established early on in the first few chapters that when God said, "let there be," it was perpetual, and He gave a portion of Himself to create everything in the universe—including man. He placed a special endowment of Himself into man when He breathed the breath of life into him, and man "Became." The word *came* is past tense, meaning that what was in the mind of God concerning man before the creation of the world was met with purpose in that moment, and man began to exist—or to *BE!* This excites me when I think of the magnificence of God and His creation. How is it that we are the salt of the earth? I am glad you asked!

> *Except a man be born of water and of the Spirit, he cannot enter into the kingdom of God. That which is born of the flesh is flesh; and that which is born of the Spirit is spirit.*
> **—John 3:5–6**

THE BE ATTITUDES

These are the words of Jesus to Nicodemus.

For there are three that bear record in heaven: the Father, the Word [who is Jesus], and the Holy Ghost: and these three are one. And there are three that bear witness in earth, the Spirit, and the water, and the blood: and these three agree in one.

—1 John 5:7–8

Being born of water and Spirit according to the Kingdom of God refers to accepting Jesus into our hearts, and the work of the cross whereby He was crucified and shed His blood for the washing away of our sins. Because He did so, the Holy Spirit causes a regeneration, or a new birth, of our spirit into the Spirit. We become born again.

Therefore if any man be in Christ, he is a new creature: old things are passed away; behold, all things are become new.

—2 Corinthians 5:17

When we accept Jesus into our lives, the washing away of our sins, as well as the continual reading of His Word, keeps an equilibrium of this spiritual water in our lives. According to His Word, we are sealed by the Holy Spirit, who is our gift from God, for receiving Jesus into our lives. He serves as our *Paraclete*, or Helper, Keeper, and Comforter, here in the earth. When we fully receive Him into our lives, we become immersed into an ever-flowing water supply of God's Word and the indwelling of

SAVORY SEASONINGS

His Spirit. The Holy Spirit, who dwells inside of us, is the Preserver of our souls. This is what causes us to become the salt or the preservative in the earth. When we allow ourselves to be totally yielded to His guidance, our lives will flourish with the love of God in our hearts, and the ability to spread the good news of Jesus Christ to others concerning the work of the cross, and the shedding of His blood for the remission of our sins.

This good news is what preserves the lives of others as they, too, share in this great experience of being born again. When we share the knowledge and experience of this great salvation, and the good news that we are no longer a slave to sin, we are sprinkling spiritual salt into the lives of others. As we study God's Word and allow the Holy Spirit to guide us in ministering this word, as we give testimony of our own deliverance from the bondage of sin, we are literally used as salt in the earth to mankind. The more seasoned we become, the more anointed by the Holy Spirit, the more the yokes in others' lives are broken, and they, too, begin to experience the salvation freely given to us when we accept Jesus into our lives as our Lord and Savior.

Thank You, Jesus, for paying the ransom for Your children with Your shed blood, as You hung on the cross for our sins.

And they overcame him by the blood of the Lamb, and by the word of their testimony; and they loved not their lives unto the death.
—Revelation 12:11

It is imperative that we continue to live a life that reflects that of Christ and His Word. We are living epistles, meaning people will read the quality of our lives as professing Christ before ever considering living the lifestyle as becoming saints. If we blend in with the world, its standards, and its systems, we will lose our saltiness, or our effectiveness to affect others' lives. When the world's influence causes us to lose sight of what we believe according to the principle of God's Word, it weakens our testimony of God's great salvation and deliverance in our lives. When we choose to remain silent to blend in with the status quo, we lose our respect as becoming children of God. This causes us to lose our relationship with God our Father by choosing the world's system by default, thereby becoming flavorless, or salt that has lost its savor.

During my research for this book, I found two reasons that fit this scenario of why salt loses its savor. The first is when it becomes contaminated with chemical impurities. An external chemical can alter or change the original purity of the salt. When we allow ourselves to become infiltrated with the ideologies of how the world view things, calling good evil and evil good, taking the Word of God and trying to counterfeit it with doctrines of men used by devils, this infiltration causes a split in our souls. We become lukewarm and double-minded, and soon this is reflected by having double standards in our lives.

So then because thou art lukewarm, and neither cold nor hot, I will spue thee out of my mouth.

—Revelation 3:16

The second reason for salt losing its savor is when it absorbs humidity and evaporates, leaving behind a substance that look likes salt but does not taste like it. We can easily see how this occurrence in the natural compares to our spiritual lives, when we allow the systems of this world to sway us into its way of doing things. Our conversations concerning the gospel of Jesus Christ are watered down. We can still look like salt, as we go to church, go through the motions, but in actuality, we are no longer affecting the world as the salt of the earth. We have, indeed, lost our savor.

And be not conformed to this world: but be ye transformed by the renewing of your mind, that ye may prove what is that good, and acceptable, and perfect, will of God.

—Romans 12:2

Father, we thank You for making the choice for us to be filled with Your Holy Spirit and for calling us according to the purpose You planned for our lives. We repent of our sins, for choosing the world over the grace You have extended toward us. Renew us and refresh us to good works so others will be able to see Your glory in our lives again, causing them to come to You for salvation, healing, and

THE BE ATTITUDES

deliverance. Cause a revival to take place in our hearts and minds that will continue into an overflowing stream, so that others may see, acknowledge, and come to drink from the rivers of life springing up in our souls by the Holy Spirit. In Jesus' name. Amen.

> *And he shall be like a tree planted by the rivers of water, that bringeth forth his fruit in his season; his leaf also shall not wither; and whatsoever he doeth shall prosper.*
>
> **—Psalm 1:3**

Father, we pray for the church as a whole. We repent as Your body of Christ for not leading by example and for allowing the gospel to be watered down by self-indulgence. We pray that You would restore everything, including "the years the locust hath eaten, the cankerworm, and the caterpillar, and the palmerworm," as You said in Joel 2:25. We pray for the savor as being the salt of the earth, the preservers of mankind, to be restored back to Your fivefold ministry—the apostles, prophets, evangelists, pastors, and teachers—and to the laymen. Increase Your power and glory in us and through us, so that we may lead others, all whom You will call to Your Son, Jesus Christ. In His name, we pray. Amen.

10

Beam Me Up

Ye are the light of the world. A city that is set on an hill cannot be hid. Neither do men light a candle, and put it under a bushel, but on a candlestick; and it giveth light unto all that are in the house.

—Matthew 5:14-15

In case you have ever wondered who you are, or whether you have any significance in this life, my answer to you would be the answer that God gave to me when I sought Him for my very own. He told me to take the word *significance* and break it up into these syllables: *SIGN-IF-I-CAN-CE*. Then He said to add the words *MY LIFE* in front of it and then read it slowly to myself. It reads: *My life is a sign if I can ce (see)*. He let me know that my life is like a neon sign to others. Whether we choose to live a good life according to His Word, or a bad life according to the world's system, our lives will shine as an example to others, whether good or bad. When we choose to live

THE BE ATTITUDES

according to the world, the light in us becomes a darkened light. If you're asking yourself, How can dark be light? turn the lights off in a dark room, close your eyes for a few minutes, then open them back up. The light you see is a dark light, but yet you can still see.

This oxymoron of light being dark represents having the mindset to live with the absence of God and His Word in our lives, and having made the choice of living according to the world's system, which Satan has devised. We can also accept Christ into our lives as Savior, but we refuse to allow Him to be Lord, thus clinging to a life bearing no good fruit as we continue to conform to the world's way of living. The second is the worst kind, because it sends confusing messages to the unbeliever. Either we are leading them to the cross of Christ, where they can find salvation, or we are causing them to stumble further into darkness, believing the Word to be of no effect in their lives.

> *The light of the body is the eye: therefore when thine eye is single [stayed on Jesus], thy whole body also is full of light; but when thine eye is evil, thy body also is full of darkness. Take heed therefore that the light which is in thee be not darkness. If thy whole body therefore be full of light, having no part dark, the whole shall be full of light, as when the bright shining of a candle doth give thee light.*
>
> **—Luke 11:34–36**

A candle lit in the darkest room will give light to the whole house. There is a saying that light is at the end of the tunnel. A light shining down a long,-stretched tunnel will give direction to someone who is lost. Even if you feel your light is dim, if you surrender that light to God, He is able to rekindle the fire in your heart and cause a reflection of His glory to be seen upon your life. My life is a "sign if I can ce," meaning I have to see myself as God sees me, the shining light that He created for His purpose here on the earth. If we cannot see Him in us, we will never be able to ascend to the potential He designed for our lives. Too long have we believed the lie of the enemy, which causes us to be defeated and feel we are under-purposed. It is the same lie he told Eve in the Garden—that if she would eat of the tree that God had forbidden, she would become like God. The truth is, she was made in God's image, as we are, and she was already like God. Satan caused her to believe the lie concerning her identity. It was the first form of identity theft in history. What has the enemy told *you*? What lie have you believed concerning yourself?

God is light, and in Him is no darkness. The portion of Himself that He breathed into man to give Him life is that light in you. When we yield ourselves to the plan that was designed by God for our lives, that light grows. Having a prayer life that renders a close relationship with Him allows a portal to, or a stream of, His presence to surround us. Accepting Christ as our Lord and Savior and being filled with His Holy Spirit gives us full access, which then allows the fullness of His glory to enter and be seen by others in our lives. It is an exchange: We trade walking in darkness for moving into His marvelous light.

> *In the beginning was the Word, and the Word was with God, and the Word was God. The same was in the beginning with God. All things were made by him; and without him was not any thing made that was made. In him was life; and the life was the light of men. And the light shineth in darkness; and the darkness comprehended it not.*
>
> **—John 1:1–5**

The Creator of the universe is in us! That makes us neon signs of His image. Our lives, although sometimes hidden, should shine as brightly as the noonday sun when we arrive on the scene. As the power of the sun's light exuding over the horizon causes the earth to come alive and blossom, so it is spiritually when the power of God is reflected in our lives. Through prayer and our relationship with Him, the light of His glory in our lives illuminates our very being, giving life and hope as we share it with others. Our lives are like neon signs pointing others to life, peace, hope, and joy, all of which comes from the Hope of glory, Jesus Christ, our Lord. By simply giving our testimony of the encounters, relationship, love, grace, and mercy that He has shown to us, we become His extended hands and the proof of His continual presence and power here on earth. By staying connected to Him through His Word, we become the outsource that He uses in the earth to show others the way. As we stay connected, we have access to His power, which is imperative, for He is the Source of all things in heaven and on earth.

For in him we live, and move, and have our being; as certain also of your poets have said, For we are also his offspring.

—Acts 17:28

Not being connected to the Source is like having an extension cord and not plugging it into the electrical outlet. The cord may look great, but it is of no use without a connection to the power source. Although it may have many cords plugged into it (representing network connections), unless it is plugged itself into the main power source—Jesus Christ—it is to no righteous avail.

I am the true vine, and my Father is the husbandman. Abide in me, and I in you. As the branch cannot bear fruit of itself, except it abide in the vine; no more can ye, except ye abide in me.

—John 15: 1, 4

Whether you are just coming to Christ, or you have known Him for many years, your testimony is unique, and it is vital in the Kingdom of God. Each of us has been assigned to a platform, on different levels, as He has chosen to reach others for the Kingdom of heaven. There is a light in you, given to you by God, along with giftings to equip you for the journey of being a light to the world.

Imagine a firefly in the dark. Though its light is tiny, it brightens an entire area of its surroundings. Not only does the light shine and expel the darkness, but its beauty is illuminated, including the magnificence of God, His wisdom, and how He creates everything in a unique way to bring glory to His name. The little firefly becomes a neon sign to all, pointing to its Creator as being awesome in all His ways. That firefly is beautiful in and of itself, but its greatest glory is seen when its surroundings are only darkness.

God's intention for you and me is to be our unique selves, to utilize every gift He has given to us, and to become that neon sign, letting our light shine among men that they may see our good works and glorify our Father in heaven. You've got this! Remember: "I can do all things through Christ which strengtheneth me" (Philippians 4:13). There is strength for the journey and sufficiency in Him. When we receive Christ into our lives, and we allow Him to become the Lord of our lives, we mimic His good works of being obedient to the Father and God's will for His life. Reading His Word, which cannot be emphasized too much, praying for the interpretation, and discerning the divine revelation of His plan of salvation for our lives helps us to learn of His ways, as well as the principles of living a productive life according to the Kingdom of God. As we pray and study His Word, the Holy Spirit guides us into all truth. This truth becomes a beacon light, showing us the ways of heaven.

> *Thy word is a lamp unto my feet, and a light unto my path.*
>
> **—Psalm 119:105**

This is the same light that emanates from us as we share His Word with others, teaching them the principles of God. Because no man can see or understand the things of God unless he is born again, our lives, when lived according to His Word, become a conduit by which others can partake of heaven and the things of God. The power of God can be seen, felt, and heard through our conversations and our writings about the Kingdom of God. It is a phenomenon that only God Himself can cause to happen in our lives. Man's word alone will stand stagnant unless the Holy Spirit breathes life into it according to His Word. This life is eternal and can only be understood through divine revelation by the Holy Spirit. This divine revelation enters our hearts and minds and causes transformation.

> *The entrance of thy words giveth light; it giveth understanding unto the simple.*
>
> **—Psalm 119:30**

Our light is needed to show others the way. The blessing He bestows upon us, both naturally and spiritually, gives light to others. When they see the children of God thriving—despite their circumstances, the economy, or the needs in their lives—it gets attention. The spotlight of

THE BE ATTITUDES

eternal blessings, divine healing, supernatural adaptability, and contentment despite overwhelming circumstances opens the door of acceptance to those experiencing these things without God in their lives. When the world is in chaos, and yet they see peace, love, joy, and a neon light that says, "Follow us to Jesus—He is the Way, the Truth, and the Life that you need," they will readily come. The world loves its own and recognizes its own by their deeds. When we allow the light of God to shine through our lives, it cannot be hidden. It is recognizable as being foreign. The standards of God are as different as night and day. With the world being darkness, and the Kingdom of God being light, it is seen wherever we go. We are in this world, but not of this world. We are in this world, but our citizenship is in heaven. The glory, giftings, and anointing on our lives all point to God and resonate in the supernatural realm.

> *God is a Spirit: and they that worship him must worship him in spirit and in truth.*
>
> **—John 4:24**

After receiving truth, or Jesus Christ, into our lives, we are changed. It is our spirit man that connects with the Holy Spirit and transcends us into heavenly places in eternity. Earth is only a temporal provision until we transition to our heavenly home. Because this is a temporary convenience given to us as we follow the plan of God, we must not allow our light to become dimmed by the world's system. Now, more than ever, is the time to seek the one and only true, wise God, with all our heart, mind, and soul, so that He may reveal to us the plan for our lives in this generation. The elders in Christ must pour into the younger ones, so that a solid foundation, and a pure light without contamination, dilution, manipulation, and deception, can be seen and procured. We must direct them back to the cross!

To those who have been hidden, God has saved us for such a time as this, as the salt of the earth, to preserve the standards of the Kingdom of God for this generation. Many altars other than those to God almighty, our Father in heaven, have been raised to worship the idols of this world. We must take a stand for righteousness and succor those whom God has chosen for the end-time harvest. The light of God, as we have experienced through our relationship with Him, must be shared with others. The divine encounters of His glory, the wonders of His majesty, with supernatural healings, miracles, signs, and wonders, must be revived and shone forth in the Church. God has saved us for such a time as this to bridge the gap in this generation. No longer can we stay hidden. God is calling us out of exile.

Arise, shine; for thy light is come, and the glory of the LORD is risen upon thee.

—Isaiah 60:1

Heavenly Father, thank You for Your glory yet shining through our lives. We accept the call to rise. We accept the mission to let our lights shine before men that they may see our good works and glorify You, our Father in heaven.

THE BE ATTITUDES

Strengthen us for the journey, redeem the time, and restore unto us, the Church, boldness, tenacity, compassion, and a burden for souls. Stir up every gift in us that has been lying dormant, and those that You have not yet revealed and chosen, to bring forth in this last dispensation of time for the end-time harvest. Create a "roar" in us to proclaim the gospel of Jesus Christ to a dying world like never before. Let Your glory rise upon us with signs, wonders, demonstrations of power, healing, and deliverance like never before. Cause the hearts of the fathers to return to the children, and the generational curses transferred onto the children by the fathers' sins to be broken, in the name of Jesus. Let God arise and His enemies be scattered in our lives and in the Church in Jesus' name! Holy Spirit, we submit ourselves unto You for divine guidance as we enter this next phase of Your glory. Our hearts, wills, souls, minds, and bodies, we submit to You to use us for Your divine purpose, to usher in the latter glory to be revealed in the earth in these last times. Help us to be vessels of honor and not dishonor, vessels bearing the brightness of Your light, and not a false light pretending truth. Examine our lives and show us where the enemy has infiltrated so that we might repent of our sins and submit that area of disobedience to You. Purify us so that the glory You are about to reveal to those who follow You may shine through us in its fullness and brightness, even as Your coming will be when You return. In Jesus' name, amen.

To all who share this same sentiment, pray this prayer in a personal way for your own life.

11

The Light of His Glory

*Let your light so shine before men that they may
see your good works, and glorify your
Father which is in heaven.*

—Matthew 5:16

This is a personal invitation from our Lord and Savior, Jesus Christ, letting us know we are accepted in the beloved. We are His children, His workmanship, His glorious chosen ones whom He has ordained and to whom He has given His glory and authority to represent the Kingdom of God in this dark world. How exciting it is to know He has put His trust in us as earthen vessels to show forth the glory of His coming Kingdom.

*For God, who commanded the light to shine
out of darkness, hath shined in our hearts, to
give the light of the knowledge of the glory
of God in the face of Jesus Christ. But we
have this treasure in earthen vessels, that the*

excellency of the power may be of God, and not of us.

—2 Corinthians 4:6–7

We belong to the Creator and Sustainer of the universe!

To the praise of the glory of his grace, wherein he hath made us accepted in the beloved.

—Ephesians 1:6

I cannot say enough about the power of the Holy Spirit that resides in us to do great exploits, as Jesus did while He was on earth. The same power that raised Christ from the dead is the same power that dwells within us. We are ambassadors of the highest Kingdom on the earth—*the Kingdom of God!* I am repeating this because to know whose you are, and who you are, is the key to allowing the light of God to shine through our lives. If we do not know the Author of the mission, or our position in the mission, we will not be able to identify ourselves to others who are apart from the mission.

In this journey, every one of us is assigned a group—a tribe, a community, a nation, a sphere, a marketplace, or even a space—where no one else can reach people but you. You are the candle in this dark world! "Let your light shine before men," He said—He made it personal. It became you and Him at that moment. It is through you that He wants to shine His glory so that others may be reached. Those to whom you are assigned will see your light, whereas

THE LIGHT OF HIS GLORY

others cannot see them. Their spiritual eyes will only be illuminated by your light because God has assigned them to you. If you have ever desired to be used by God, this is the most opportune time the world has ever known. There is a verse of Scripture that says, "My heart is indicting a good matter: I speak of the things which I have made touching the king: my tongue is the pen of a ready writer" (Psalm 45:1). Now is the time to rise out of obscurity. Everything God has shared, through word and deed, must be proclaimed so that His glory may be revealed in and through us in these end times.

There is a clarion call for the remnant to arise and shine so that others may see the way to the cross. In a world where good is being called evil and evil is being called good, we must take a stand and be the line of demarcation so others can know the difference and choose that which is good.

The power of God is not limited. I am a firm believer that these latter days will be greater than the former: greater in quantity because we can never supersede the quality in which Christ showed forth the Kingdom of God. That which we have seen will not compare to what is to come. If we allow our light to shine, or the power of the Holy Spirit to flow through us without any reservations, God will manifest Himself through us like never before.

THE BE ATTITUDES

Jesus Christ the same yesterday, and to day, and for ever.

—Hebrews 13:8

If Moses was used to part the Red Sea so the children of Israel could cross on dry land, to strike the rock in the wilderness and bring forth water; and if Elijah was used to shut up the heavens through prayer so that it did not rain for three and a half years, then recalled the rain back into its position through prayer, then called down fire from heaven to show that God was the only true, living God; and if Joshua could command the sun to stand still and not go down until the battle was won by the power of God; and if so many other people allowed the power of God to move through their lives, then *so can we!* If they believed in and trusted God to perform it, why can't we? He loves us and is willing to use us just as powerfully as He did them. They were used in their generation, and now it is time for our generation. Let us answer the call.

Your good works is needed for this time—for this hour, for this season, and for this dispensation of glory, so the Kingdom of God will be revealed to bridge the gap for this generation, and the next, if the Lord's return has not yet occurred. As Christ sacrificed Himself, dying on the cross for our sins, being resurrected on the third day, ascending to the Father, then promising to return and receive us unto Himself, so ought we to also sacrifice, so that others may be able to partake of this same glory.

THE LIGHT OF HIS GLORY

I beseech you therefore, brethren, by the mercies of God, that ye present your bodies a living sacrifice, holy, acceptable unto God, which is your reasonable service.

—Romans 12:1

There used to be a commercial that said, "Uncle Sam needs you!" Well, the Father God needs *you* to carry out His will here on the earth. All He needs is a willing vessel—He will do the rest. If you have not already done so, receive Christ into your life, and say yes to His will. As you communicate with Him through prayer, surrender yourself to the cause of Christ to further the commission to tell others about Him, and the price He paid for our sins.

Good works come through the repentance of our sins or by asking God for the forgiveness of our sins and turning away from them. Accepting Christ as our Lord and Savior and acknowledging the work of the cross, where He willingly shed His blood, and by dying there on that cross as a living sacrifice, He paid the penalty for our sins, overcame death, hell, and the grave, ascended on high to the Father, gave gifts unto men (us), giving us (the believer) the power to become the sons of God and to operate under the same power and authority that Jesus did while here on earth. Allowing the Holy Spirit to work in us and through us will manifest that power and authority given to us as ambassadors of Christ so that others might see and believe. Just as Jesus demonstrated the power of God through His life in order for God to be revealed and glorified to the

THE BE ATTITUDES

unbeliever, so it will be when we, the sons of God, take our given position here on earth, having dominion over the power of darkness.

As children of light, we are to illuminate or make visible the Kingdom of God through our lives. In order to be effective, we ourselves must be partakers first by studying the Word of God—not just the printed Word, but a relationship with the living Word, which is Jesus Christ, our Lord. Studying His ways and His teachings concerning the Kingdom of God fills our lives with the illumination, or light, of God and His Kingdom. We are only a reflection of the true Light as He shines his glory through our lives. It's a continuation of His divine work manifesting in us and through us. Because of the corruption and evil of this world, the true gospel has been watered down to fit in with society's hustle and bustle, its way of doing things. We have almost lost a generation, and this has caused a great gap in the true teachings and way of life that Christ would have in the Church. As sad as it may sound, however, all hope is not lost. God has always kept for Himself a remnant who stayed true to His Word. That remnant includes you and me, and all who will say and are still saying yes to His will! We have work to do. There is a people who need Your light to shine. We must teach the true Word of God to this generation and demonstrate it with power by the Holy Spirit that they may know that God is not dead, but is very much alive, and Jesus is still reigning as the King of kings and Lord of lords!

THE LIGHT OF HIS GLORY

Light can be referred to as a symbol of understanding and intellectual thought, and it is the opposite of ignorance, or darkness. The Word says, "My people are destroyed for lack of knowledge: because thou hast rejected knowledge, I will also reject thee, that thou shalt be no priest to me: seeing thou hast forgotten the law of thy God, I will also forget thy children" (Hosea 4:6).

Knowing that without having the truth of the Word of God in their lives would cause them to perish saddens the heart of God. This is why He needs you and me, and all who are willing to join Him in this last outpouring of glory to gather this end-day harvest. We must teach and preach the truth of His Word, so that light would come.

> *The entrance of thy words giveth light; it giveth understanding unto the simple.*
> **—Psalm 119:130**

> *Thy word is a lamp unto my feet, and a light unto my path.*
> **—Psalm 119:105**

God is asking, "Will you take a stand with Me today? Will you allow Me to show Myself strong through your life today? Will you help show others the way to salvation?"

The call of God to help glorify His name throughout the earth is the greatest honor offered to man. The almighty God, Maker of heaven and earth, is offering us the opportunity to join with Him to help save a dying world, one soul at a time. Uncle Sam calls for others to join the cause to help save a nation, but God is calling us to join His cause to help save the world. Although He is reaching out to the world, He is also a personal God, and He is reaching out to you, to me, and to our family and friends. I am reminded of the story of Lazarus and his sisters n John 11. They were followers and friends of Jesus. Lazarus became ill, even to the point of death, and Jesus, at the call of Lazarus's sisters, went to Bethany to help them. By the time He arrived, however, Lazarus had been dead and entombed for four days. When it seemed all hope was gone and the situation was impossible, Jesus, when He first heard of the situation, said, "This sickness is not unto death, but for the glory of God, that the Son of God might be glorified thereby" (John 11:4). When He arrived at the scene, after talking with Mary and Martha, He went to the gravesite. He prayed to the Father and said, "Father, I thank thee that thou hast heard me. And I knew that thou hearest me always: but because of the people which stand by I said it, that they may believe that thou hast sent me" (verses 41–42). He then said, "Lazarus, come forth," and the dead came forth. (Please read the eleventh chapter of John for the full story.)

This display of action showed several things, but to point out a few: First, Jesus' position was as the Son of God, as a personal friend, but far more, as a conduit and carrier of the power and glory of God. And this is one of many examples where He displayed the principle of letting our light shine before others so that they may see our good

THE LIGHT OF HIS GLORY

works and glorify the Father in heaven. We are the sons of God, adopted in God's family by Jesus Christ, and given the inheritance of all that belong to Him, including the authority of His name to do the same works that He did to continue the mission of our Father.

God has sanctioned you and me, in a good way, to carry on this glorious crusade of displaying the Kingdom of God here on earth, so that others may hear, see, and believe on His name. Just as He was concerned about Lazarus and his family, so is He concerned about our personal lives and all those who are near and dear to us. He has given a promise to those who believe that He will save us and our households. Allowing the light of God to shine through our lives will cause an immediate response to those who knew us before Christ, compared to the new man in Christ that they are now witnessing. The change will be undeniable. Whether it be a sparkle, as the firefly in the night, or a floodlight coming straight from heaven, the light of God will be seen in our lives.

It is such a glorious time in history. It is a time when the coming of the Lord could happen any day! Every lighthouse, spotlight, candle, or whatever light you are carrying should be lit to its full capacity, pointing the way to Christ before His return. If you have used up the oil in your lamp, purchase some more and prune the wick through fasting and prayer, so that you will be able to see the Bridegroom when He comes! Let the light of God shine through your life like never before and receive your reward

THE BE ATTITUDES

of blessings from God.

God's glory cannot be compared to anything else on earth. It even excels the brightness of the noonday sun. He is the Creator and the Sustainer of the whole universe; therefore, if everything is dependent upon Him for its survival, nothing is equivalent or can compare to Him. This in itself shows His magnificence, majesty, magnanimity, multifaceted greatness—and the list can go on forever, because He is, was, and is to come. His glory is best seen in His creation. There are no two things in the universe created by Him that are alike! Tell me, who else do you know who can carry that credential truthfully? Whether in heaven, on earth, or under the sea, all things were created by Him, uniquely designed with a purpose to live out in this world. How awesome is that to try to fathom? I stand in complete awe when I think about the power of His glory when He spoke those three words at creation: "Let there be!" Although God, in His infinite wisdom, created everything on the earth, it was because of His love for us that He designed it so that we might share in His glory.

How do I know this? When God created man, it was after He had laid out everything for his provision and protection, his survival while on the earth. He then created Adam and gave him dominion over everything He had created for him. He also gave him the task to exercise his God-given abilities, as he named everything that he encountered here on the earth. The ability to name them showed God's glory manifesting through his life. The diversity of God's creation

THE LIGHT OF HIS GLORY

did not devastate him, but rather, it intensified his ability to show forth his creativity —in his Father's image. He was mirroring the wisdom, knowledge, and understanding for the purpose for which they were created, and their function on the earth. Today this is called science, and it involves discovering the different functions and purposes of the various things that God has created and placed on the earth for our pleasure. Adam had a deeper understanding of creation because of his continual sharing of God's Presence and glory. He was able to see himself through his creator on a level that we as children of God should seek to know.

God loves us so much. He thrives on us being in His Presence to experience the glory that He placed inside of us, that being a portion of Himself. If we would only tap into the God that is in us, we would be amazed at the power and authority in His name that He has given to us as becoming saints. To experience His glory in the same fashion as Adam—I believe this is the next phase of the revelation knowledge that He is giving to man in this next dispensation and dimension of time. He is visiting with us in His full glory on the earth, as He did with Adam, bringing all things back full circle, including His communion and Presence with His people, those who are the called according to His purpose. I am so excited to see His glory in this magnitude in the earth. Not only do I want to see it, but I want to be a full participant in this outpouring and the reaping of the harvest in this time.

As we discover the God in us, as Adam did, and we

THE BE ATTITUDES

allow Him to stir up the light within us, or our God-given abilities, according to the power and authority that He has invested in us, we will recognize that we are the beacons of light that our Father created to dominate and reveal His Presence and power throughout the earth. We are to be the neon sign in the earth, pointing the way to heaven. We are to be the light in this dark world. Notice I said "*in* this world"; we are not the Light *of* this world. Only Jesus and He alone holds that position. When we try to be the light *of* someone's life, instead of being the light *in* someone's life, we automatically set ourselves up to be overtaken by Satan with pride. When Jesus said we are the "light of the world," He was speaking concerning His return to the Father and our position as His ambassadors in the earth, pointing others to the way of the true Light, or Himself. As Adam found that disobedience and separation from God created a life filled with darkness, so it is for those who choose their own way. Let us meditate on the goodness and glory of God and all of creation so that we are honored to serve a loving God like this. Let us seek ways to allow our lives to become a light to others, pointing out the awesome God we serve and His love for all mankind. Lastly, let us seek to know Him in the power of His might and His presence, which will bring the same glory into our lives as it did for Adam. We will discover the light in us and have dominion over every obstacle that prevents us from letting our light shine so that others may see who we are in God, and even more importantly, who they can become as they yield their lives to Him. As we yield our own lives to Him and remain

THE LIGHT OF HIS GLORY

in His Presence, all will recognize His glory upon us as He moves and works through us. As Moses' face lit up with the glory of God after being in His Presence, so will ours. As we extend His love to others through our gifts, our forgiveness of others, our love, our patience, and our true compassion, the glory of God will rest upon our lives. As we keep communion with Him through prayer, reading His Word, fasting, and showing His mercy to others, the weight of His glory will rest upon us like a cloak. Its called a mantle, just like Elijah's mantle, which rested upon him.

Having access to this glory makes us an eternal blessing to others. As a conduit of the blessing, we ourselves cannot help but to also receive the blessings as they flow through us. Having an open hand, giving to others, and allowing access to ourselves through ministering to and counseling others ensures a continuous blessing in our lives. As we delight ourselves in Him, He will also personalize the blessing by giving us the desires of our hearts. It is a win-win situation, especially because we are on the winning team! Allowing God's glory to rest upon us, to be used in the deliverance of and impartation to others, causes us to dwell in the shadow of the Almighty. It serves as our resting place.

> *He that dwelleth in the secret place of the most High shall abide under the shadow of the Almighty. I will say of the LORD, He is my refuge and my fortress: my God; in him will I trust.*

> **—Psalm 91:1–2**

THE BE ATTITUDES

In this secret place, we are given divine revelations of the Kingdom of heaven by the Holy Spirit, and sometimes we experience divine encounters, such as divine visitations of angels, things of heaven, and even Jesus Himself. I count it a privilege and an honor to be a glory carrier and distributor of heaven's blessings, sharing the gospel of Jesus Christ and His manifested glory through my life.

You may be wondering how we can do good works that glorify our Father in heaven. After reading all the above explanations, the next thing to do is simply to begin—if you have not already—witnessing to others of the life of Jesus Christ as you know it. Tell them of the cross, its purpose, and how believing and receiving Jesus' sacrifice for us can change their lives. Tell them of His soon return and the importance of receiving Him now. Give your own personal testimony of how He has changed your life, and how He is still working personally in your circumstances.

> *And they overcame him by the blood of the Lamb, and by the word of their testimony; and they loved not their lives unto the death.*
>
> **—Revelation 12:11**

If you are in the ministry, begin to pray for the Holy Spirit to manifest Himself through your life with signs, wonders, and miracles, so that others may see and know that God is real, and that Jesus is still alive, working in and through the lives of His people. Live a holy life before all, setting a standard for righteousness for the people to see

THE LIGHT OF HIS GLORY

and know the difference between good and evil. Teach the Word of God by revelation knowledge from the Holy Spirit (*rhema*). Stay in communion with God through prayer and reading His Word. Fast to strengthen your inner man (your spirit), so that you may be able to hear clearly what the Holy Spirit is saying, and which direction He is leading you in these last days.

If you need to pray the sinners' prayer, repeat these words: *Father, I thank You for my life. Forgive me for my sins and for living according to this world. I believe that Your Son, Jesus, died for my sins, and that through His death and resurrection, I can now be reconciled back to You and the Kingdom of God. I receive You, Jesus, as my Lord and Savior. Come into my life and teach me Your ways. I receive the gift of the Holy Spirit. Spirit, breathe upon me now, in Jesus' name. Amen.*

Welcome into the Kingdom of God! As Jesus has said:

> *Behold, I stand at the door, and knock: if any man hear my voice, and open the door, I will come in to him, and will sup with him, and he with me.*

—Revelation 3:20

God's Word also tells us:

> *If thou shalt confess with thy mouth the Lord Jesus, and shalt believe in thine heart that God hath raised him from the dead, thou shalt be*

THE BE ATTITUDES

saved. For with the heart man believeth unto righteousness; and with the mouth confession is made unto salvation.

—Romans 10:9–10

You are now accepted in the beloved, and you no longer are a servant of sin. God has given you the power to conquer the sin in your life in the name of Jesus.

But as many as received him, to them gave he power to become the sons of God, even to them that believe on his name: which were born, not of blood, nor of the will of the flesh, nor of the will of man, but of God.

—John 1:12–13

You are now born again! Find a full-gospel Bible-teaching church; pray always; and read God's Word for instruction. Seek the Holy Spirit through prayer for divine direction. May God bless you!

Here is a prayer for the believer: *Father, I thank You now for Your goodness and the mercy that You have shown toward me. Thank You for Your precious Son, Jesus, whose sacrifice allowed me to be accepted in the beloved. I now am a joint-heir of the Kingdom of heaven with Him. Thank You, Lord, for all things in Christ that concern my life. Thank You, Jesus, for salvation, healing, and deliverance in my life. Thank You for allowing me to be a light in this dispensation of time and to be a glory carrier to show forth Your signs, wonders, and miracles to this generation. I*

THE LIGHT OF HIS GLORY

willingly accept my responsibility to share Your Word to others in this season. Thank You for every blessing in my life as I strive to represent You and the Kingdom according to Your Word. Let those whom You have assigned to me open their hearts and be conditioned by the Holy Spirit to receive Your Word. Allow our destinies to cross and give us discernment to know Your divine will for our lives. Thank You for divine connections.

Thank You, Jesus, for all You have done in the lives of Your people. We are eternally grateful to be called and chosen by You to carry out Your plans in the earth. We anticipate Your glory to be revealed as we patiently await Your return. In Your name we pray. Maranatha!

12

Comprehension Review

(For additional space, you may use the
section listed as notes.)

Chapter 1: Blessings of the Kingdom of Heaven

When was the word *be* first mentioned in the Bible? What
were at least three of its meanings?

_____

_____

_____

_____

Name at least three ways we can be poor in spirit.

_____

_____

What is spiritual poverty?

_____

_____

THE BE ATTITUDES

Chapter 2: Comforting Thoughts

Name three areas of mourning.

_____

_____

What is spiritual mourning?

_____

_____

How do we comfort ourselves and others?

_____

_____

Chapter 3: The Inheritance of the Meek

What is considered meekness in Matthew 5?

_____

_____

Should the Church be silent concerning immorality in order to have meekness?

_____

_____

COMPREHENSION REVIEW

How is meekness a condition of the heart?

_____

_____

Chapter 4: Filled to the Brim

In your own words, explain how you fill yourself up with righteousness.

_____

_____

How is our true identity stored? (Hint: It is in the part of us that longs for God.)

_____

_____

When we hunger and thirst for righteousness, what is the bread that feeds us?

_____

_____

Chapter 5: Unlimited Mercy

Share a brief incident in which you showed mercy.

_____

_____

THE BE ATTITUDES

Name three ways God shows mercy.

In what ways can we mirror God's character by showing mercy to others?

What is the importance of forgiveness?

Make a list of all those whom you have not forgiven.

Chapter 6: Pure Eyesight

Name three virtues that keep us pure.

What is the reward for being pure in heart?

COMPREHENSION REVIEW

How do we keep our minds pure?

_____

_____

Chapter 7: Blessings of Peace

Do you consider yourself to be a peacemaker? If so, list three ways you engage in peacemaking. If not, list the reasons you believe you are not a peacemaker.

_____

_____

_____

_____

What are three things to overcome in order to become an effective peacemaker?

_____

_____

Chapter 8: Righteous Blessings, Destiny Helpers

What is your reaction when you are talked about, belittled, and lied about by others?

_____

_____

THE BE ATTITUDES

What did Jesus do when He was faced with these same tests?

_____

_____

Name three spirits that can cause bitterness to enter your heart.

_____

_____

What virtue conquers a multitude of sins? (Hint: Jesus said we should do this to our enemies.)

_____

_____

Chapter 9: Savory Seasonings

What does the phrase "Ye are the salt of the earth" mean?

_____

_____

How does our spiritual salt lose its savor?

_____

_____

COMPREHENSION REVIEW

How can we preserve others' lives for Christ?

_____

_____

Chapter 10: Beam Me Up

When you break the word *significance* into syllables, what phrase do you see?

_____

_____

How are we neon signs in the earth?

_____

_____

Can the light in us ever become dark? Explain your answer.

_____

_____

What should we do to brighten our light?

_____

_____

Chapter 11: The Light of His Glory

Amidst all the things going on in the world, how can we let our light shine?

_____

_____

What are our good works? Can we work too much and leave God out of our efforts?

_____

_____

Name the incident in the Bible about which Jesus said, "This sickness is not unto death, but for the glory of God, that the Son of God might be glorified thereby."

_____

_____

How did Jesus glorify God in this incident?

_____

_____

How do we glorify God in our own lives today?

_____

_____

Epilogue

The attitudes we have as becoming believers will reflect our hearts and show forth our true character. When we name the name of Christ, we are expected by others to present a life lived as mirrored and reflective of godly principles, according to the Word of God and the life Jesus lived before us while He was on the earth.

> *God is a Spirit: and they that worship him must worship him in spirit and in truth.*
>
> **—John 4:24**

The Spirit is sometimes compared to a prism because of its transparency and its ability to reflect light in multifaceted ways, including in many different colors. God used the rainbow as a symbol to Noah that He would not flood the earth again in that manner:

> *I have set my rainbow in the clouds, and it will be the sign of the covenant between me and the earth. Whenever I bring clouds over the earth and the rainbow appears in the clouds, I will remember my covenant between me and you and all living creatures of every kind. Never again will the waters become a flood to destroy all life, Whenever the rainbow appears in the clouds, I will see it and remember the everlasting covenant*

THE BE ATTITUDES

between God and all living creatures of every kind on the earth.

—Genesis 9:13–16

So, colors have value in the spirit realm. We will use these colors as attitudes, or attributes, of the Father. The way our attitudes as the "Church" are portrayed to others when we experience tests and trials can be reflected as colors that sway how we affect our generation and those with whom we come in contact. No matter our titles or positions, or even being just a believer, the life we choose to live will either cause an overflow of blessings promised to us, and victory over Satan, or cause the opposite effect in our lives. The Beatitudes passage, found in Matthew 5, tells of Jesus teaching His disciples and followers the principles to having a blessed life. Starting out on His God-given mission to fulfill the Scriptures prophesied of Him, and to set in motion the plan of salvation, Jesu sat upon a hill and taught them. Afterward, he began His journey to live what He had just taught by example. Not only did He speak the Word, teaching the Word, but He lived the Word. These were lessons taught and instilled by being a living example to all who were present as they were on their journey. He became a living epistle, a neon sign, a spotlight referring to the power of God and the Kingdom of heaven.

The people which sat in darkness saw great light; and to them which sat in the region and shadow of death light is sprung up.

—Matthew 4:16

EPILOGUE

As I was reading these two chapters, it was as if my eyes began to open in another lens, and the Scriptures began to unfold into what I call the "proceedings," or the preamble of Jesu's life being unveiled to them. Right then and there, He mapped out His own life before them. He was teaching them what to do in a crisis, in certain life situations, to reap a harvest of blessings, and to obtain the victory in every area of their lives, all while glorifying the Father in heaven and carrying out His plans in the earth. Its no wonder that He is the King of kings and the Lord of lords.

> *Wherefore he saith, When he ascended up on high, he led captivity captive, and gave gifts [blessings] unto men.*
>
> **—Ephesians 4:8**

The enemy cannot take away your blessing, but he can cause you to disqualify yourself for the blessing if your attitudes are not reflective of Christ as becoming saints. However, when you choose to follow Jesus' life pattern and live according to the principles in these BE Attitudes, inspired by the Holy Spirit according to Matthew 5, the promise of blessings will overtake you.

> *For all the promises of God in him are yea, and in him Amen, unto the glory of God by us.*
>
> **—2 Corinthians 1:20**

The sum total, as we allow the Holy Spirit to arise in and through our lives in this hour, is that not only will the world see our light shining, but the world is about to see

THE BE ATTITUDES

His glory in a new light as the outpouring of His glory upon the sons of God begins to flow and manifest in our lives, both naturally and spiritually. The oil that burns inside of you is about to be magnified in exponential proportions. You are about to *Be-come* a beacon of light. The unveiling has begun. The outpouring of blessings shall overtake you in this season.

> *Arise, shine, for thy light is come, and the glory of the LORD is risen upon thee. For, behold, the darkness shall cover the earth, and gross darkness the people: but the LORD shall arise upon thee, and his glory shall be seen upon thee. And the Gentiles shall come to thy light, and kings to the brightness of thy rising.*
>
> **—Isaiah 60:1–3**

Let the light of God shine so that others will see and recognize that the same God who said, "Let there be light," is the same God who is working through your life. Speak life into others. The power of life and death is in your tongue. The same creative power that said, "Let there be light," was given unto us, the believers.

> *Death and life are in the power of the tongue: and they that love it shall eat the fruit thereof.*
>
> **—Proverbs 18:21**

In the name of Jesus, let it be so. Amen!

About the Author

Murle Jones is an ordained evangelist, author, playwright producer, and philanthropist. She is also the founder of Beams of Heaven Ministries located in Memphis, Tennessee. Beams of Heaven is a ministry committed to teaching the gospel to others and building up the body of Christ. Murle is dedicated to bridging the gap for this generation by unveiling truths of His Word and living the Christian life with demonstration of power, healing, and deliverance. She is also the founder of the Murle Jones Project, an umbrella outreach program that ministers to the homeless and the youth of this generation. As an extended hand of God, her ministry reaches out to the homeless and those whom most of society deems as hopeless. From the drug addict to those facing misfortune, people are offered both natural and spiritual food, as her ministry teams up with homeless shelters to offer a hand up, instead of a handout.

Murle believes that every soul created by God has great potential in life, as God has purposed. She strives to help others live out the Scripture: "'For I know the plans I have for you,' declares the LORD, 'plans to prosper you and not to harm you, plans to give you hope and a future'" (Jeremiah 29:11 NIV). Murle believes that every soul is a diamond in the rough, until it is polished with the Word of God. She knows that "the entrance of thy (God's) words giveth light; it giveth understanding unto the simple" (Psalm 119:130), and she understands that "thou shalt be a crown of glory in the hand of the LORD, and a royal diadem in the hand of thy God" (Isaiah 62:3) is a promise to all who receive Him. Her ministry reaches out to the youth, building programs to help them with their identity, which includes the study of the Word of God and stirring up their God-given creative abilities through the arts. She works to connect with communities where there is disparity, praying to turn the hearts of the fathers back to their children. Her ultimate mission is to spread the gospel to all whom the Lord will send.

> *Thank you to all who received this word. It was a pleasurable experience to be used, while allowing the Holy Spirit to pour into your life. Thank You, Jesus!*
>
> **—Murle Jones**

Notes

Notes

Notes

Notes

Notes

Notes

Notes

Notes

Notes

Notes

Ministry Information

Email: **BeamsofHeavenMinistries@gmail.com**

Email: **murlejonesproject@gmail.com**

Facebook: **murlejonesproject@gmail.com**

Instagram: **murlejonesproject@gmail.com**

Let Your Light Shine!

The Be Attitudes is a didactic writing set in motion by the Holy Spirit to revive a hunger and thirst for righteousness—a right relationship between God and man—which provokes an outpouring of blessings from an open heaven into our lives. The purpose of these writings is to edify the body of Christ, to enlighten the believer of the nature of Christ, and to assist the follower of Christ on the journey of walking in blessings as he or she portrays the life of Christ through their daily lives and walk with Him.

According to Deuteronomy 28, which I believe aligns with Matthew 5, if we follow and obey the commandments of God, according to the truth of His Word, as Jesus lived by example for us, nothing but overflowing blessings will overtake us during our journey. We will be:

Blessed in our everyday lives

Blessed in our walk with God

Blessed as the children of God

Blessed to have victory over the enemy

Blessed in every area of our lives, with nothing missing, nothing lacking.

THE BE ATTITUDES

Murle Jones is an ordained evangelist, author, playwright producer, and philanthropist. She is the founder of Beams of Heaven Ministries, located in Memphis Tennessee. Beams of Heaven is a ministry committed to teaching the gospel to others and building up the body of Christ. Murle is dedicated to bridging the gap for this generation by unveiling truths of God's Word and living the Christian life with the demonstration of power, healing, and deliverance. She is the founder of the Murle Jones Project, an umbrella outreach program that ministers to the homeless and youth of this generation.